Educational Research

Contemporary Issues
and Practical Approaches

Jerry Wellington

continuum

Continuum

The Tower Building
11 York Road
London SE1 7NX, UK

80 Maiden Lane,
Suite 704
New York, NY 10038

www.continuumbooks.com

First published 2000
Reprinted 2003 (twice), 2004, 2008

British Library Cataloguing-in-Publication Data
A catalogue record for this book is available from the British Library

ISBN 978-0-8264-4970-2 (hardback)
       978-0-8264-4971-9 (paperback)

Typeset by Paston PrePress Ltd, Beccles, Suffolk
Printed in Great Britain by the MPG Books Group, Bodmin and King's Lynn

Contents

Acknowledgements

I would like to thank all those colleagues and students whose feedback on earlier drafts of this book was so essential to the development of the manuscript, especially

Len Barton
Mick Hammond
Denise Harrison
Nicki Hedge
Gary McCulloch
Jon Scaife
Lorna Unwin.

I would also like to thank Tony Edwards for alerting me to the idea behind the cartoon in Chapter 12 and David Houchin (a student at Silverdale Comprehensive School) for drawing it.

I am especially grateful to Tina Cartwright for all her help in preparing and organizing the manuscript, the tables, the figures and the boxes.

JERRY WELLINGTON

Preface

This book has been written for anyone undertaking a research study into an aspect of education, training or a related area. It is intended primarily as an introduction, for students, teachers or beginning researchers, to the mainly qualitative methods that are often used in research work where a large-scale quantitative approach is either not affordable or not appropriate. The main focus therefore is on interview and case-study work, although survey research is discussed briefly.

There are many references to literature and further reading, including both recent publications and some of the classic writing on method which has been published since the 1950s and 1960s.

In summary, the main aim of this book is to provide an introductory guide to some of the methods and the methodology people can use in their own research, and to introduce the literature and the thinking which lies behind them.

The title of the book includes the word 'educational'; this is deliberate. My view is that research should be educational, in the sense that we can and should learn from it. This view, and the role of educational research, is discussed fully in the final chapter.

I hope that this book is readable, useful and thought-provoking. Please let me know what you think, preferably using e-mail to the following address: j.wellington@sheffield.ac.uk

ABOUT THE AUTHOR

Jerry Wellington's first degree was gained at Bristol University, where he studied Physics and Philosophy. Shortly afterwards he took a postgraduate certificate in education at the London Institute and then began a teaching career in Tower Hamlets, East London. Here he became involved in educational research as a comprehensive-school teacher, and took a part-time MA course in the Philosophy of Education, again at the London Institute. Later, he became a lecturer at the University of Sheffield, where he has taught on PGCE, Diploma, MEd, MA, PhD and EdD courses. While working at Sheffield, he has undertaken research of many different kinds: large- and small-scale; some school-based; some college-based; some looking at work-based learning; and some externally funded.

He has been involved in the writing of six books (either as author or co-author), six edited books, and 46 journal articles (some single- and some co-authored) to date. This is his fourth sole-authored book, but all of them have been stimulated by other people's writing and have been helped greatly by feedback from students and colleagues. He has also written for a wider audience, and has published articles in the *Times Educational Supplement*, teachers' bulletins and news-papers.

Part 1: Issues and Approaches

An introduction to educational research

DOING RESEARCH

Research in education can be very enjoyable. Travelling around, encountering different schools, hearing new accents, meeting employers, seeing 'how the other half live' are all part of the fun. My own research has taken me into most regions of the UK; parts of several other countries; a range of schools and City Technology Colleges (Wellington, 1993) and a number of employers of varying shapes, sizes and in different sectors (Wellington, 1989, 1993).

Research can involve asking people questions, listening and observing and evaluating resources, schemes, programmes and teaching methods. It can also be messy, frustrating and unpredictable. Conducting focus groups in which only one person turns up, arranging to meet a group of apprentices 90 miles away and arriving to find that their 'mentor' had mistakenly sent them home, visiting a school to find it closed for a 'Baker Day', arranging to interview a 'very busy' employer for half an hour and then that employer talks for two hours; all these things have happened to me.

These are the differences between educational research that deals with humans and their learning organizations, and research in physics (my original subject), which deals with inanimate, intangibles like point masses, rigid bodies and frictionless surfaces.

These differences also imply a different code of conduct. Education involves the study of human beings; the physical sciences, although having their own canons and ethics, do not make the same ethical demands as does education. Ethical concerns should be at the forefront of any research project and should continue through to the write-up and dissemination stages.

Morals and ethics in educational research are considered in a later chapter of this book. (For further discussion of ethics in social research see Robson (1993, pp. 29–35), Cohen and Manion (1994), Shipman (1988) and many other sources.)

EDUCATIONAL RESEARCH IN THE MEDIA

Educational research features constantly in the media. Education, like politics and the selection of the England soccer team, is a subject on which most people consider they are an expert (we've all been to school after all). The collage of newspaper cuttings in Figure 1.1

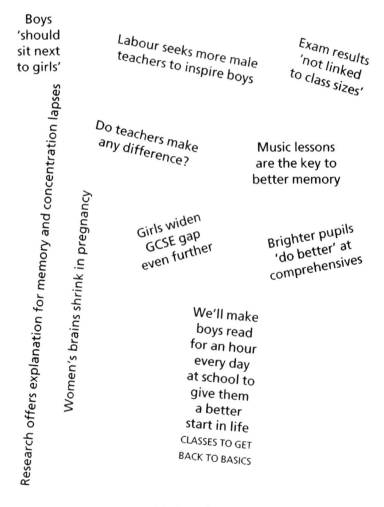

Figure 1.1: Educational research in the media

shows some of the old 'chestnuts' which have been media favourites for decades: the issue of class size compared with pupil achievement, the question of whether teachers can make a difference, and, of course, the traditional 'teacher-bashing' exercise, in which teachers are blamed for every social ill from unemployment, through soccer hooliganism, to teenage pregnancies. A more recent hot issue has been the under-achievement of boys, which received massive newspaper coverage in early 1998 and has recurred regularly since. (One wonders whether the media spotlight would have been as strong if girls' GCSE results had fallen significantly below boys'.)

Thus the School Standards Minister, via the tabloids, was urging, in January 1998, that boys should be forced to read for an hour a day, and even that boys should sit next to girls in class.

As well as the usual suspects, the occasional zany or off-the-wall item of research makes headlines. Music lessons, for example, were said, in 1998, to be the 'key to a better memory'. This conclusion was based on a 'controlled' experiment in Hong Kong involving 30 female students who had received music lessons and another 30 who had not. This research was first reported in *Nature* and it attracted newspaper interest; perhaps because it involved a controlled experiment which was perceived to have higher, or 'scientific,' status. Similarly, the observation that 'women's brains shrink during pregnancy' was based on 'new scientific evidence' published in *New Scientist* in 1997.

A systematic research programme that carried out an in-depth study of current media selection, filtering and portrayal of educational research would make an ideal project. My own suspicion is that it would reveal a media bias towards educational research which is seen as 'scientific', objective and value-free, as opposed to studies that are qualitative and therefore deemed to be value-laden and subjective.

Studies have been carried out of media coverage of specific aspects of education, e.g. Pettigrew and MacLure (1997), on the grant-maintained schools of that era; Baker (1994), on tabloid coverage of teacher unions; and Warburton and Saunders (1996), on newspaper images of teachers in the 1970s. But, to my knowledge, no systematic examination has been made of newspaper filtering and portrayal of educational research itself – a gap well worth filling.

We return to recent criticisms of educational research, in the media and elsewhere, in a later chapter and also to the public portrayal of educational research by key figures.

A BRIEF HISTORY OF EDUCATIONAL RESEARCH: RECURRENT DEBATES

A thorough study, or a detailed story, of the history of educational research would make an excellent project. We cannot do that here (although several references form good starting points[1]) but we can trace some of the key features and past definitions which have shaped its history. This brief history will help to highlight some of the recurring debates in educational research: quantitative versus qualitative approaches; the importance of ethics; the comparison with science and the so-called 'scientific method'; the connection between research and practice; differing beliefs in the nature of reality (ontology) and the way in which we acquire knowledge of it (epistemology).

The Laboratory Approach

The end of the nineteenth century saw Galton's work on the study of 'individual differences', an area which was to return more notoriously, in 1973, with Edward Jensen (see below, p. 7). Galton's work was largely laboratory based and dependent on the statistical techniques of that era (see Verma and Mallick, 1999, p. 56).

Thorndike's work, in the first quarter of the last century, is often noted as a key influence in the years to come. His famous slogan, 'Whatever exists at all exists in some amount' (Thorndike, 1918, p. 16), inspired and influenced subsequent researchers to mimic the 'scientific method' and rely exclusively on quantitative methods. His work on testing and academic achievement was also very much 'laboratory research', divorced from the messy reality of schools and classrooms – another persistent issue for debate which resurfaced in the criticisms of educational research that were a feature of the 1990s (see Chapter 12).

Despite his apparent obsession with the quantitative, and distance from the classroom (see Verma and Mallick, 1999, p. 57), Thorndike's work in one area remains, ironically, a live issue. He argued that

---

1. Bloom, B. S. (1966) 'Twenty-five years of educational research'. *American Educational Research Journal*, **3**, 212; Dennis, W. (1941) 'Infant development under conditions of restricted practice and of minimum social stimulation'. *Genetic Psychology Monographs*, **23**, 143–89; Eggleston, J. (1979) 'The characteristics of educational research; mapping the domain'. *British Educational Research Journal*, **5**(1), 1–12; Kerlinger, F. N. (1977) 'The influence of research on education practice'. *Educational Researcher*, **6**(8), 5–11; Peters, R. S. and White, J. P. (1969) 'The philosopher's contribution to educational research'. *Educational Philosophy and Theory*, **1**, 1–15.

training (or learning) in one situation would not transfer readily to another situation or context. His scepticism over 'transfer of training' is ironic in that his own conclusions on the difficulty of transfer have been extended and generalized, from the clean, clinical world of the laboratory to the complex, unpredictable worlds of school education and youth training. The transfer debate reappeared prominently in the 1970s with the emergence of 'generic' or 'transferable' skills both in schooling and youth training, based on the belief that they would make young people more employable. Skills of a similar nature were given further emphasis by the 'core skills' movement in the 1980s which renamed them 'key skills' in the 1990s. Thorndike's original scepticism reappeared in the 'situated cognition' movement of this later era, which argued persuasively that skill, knowledge and understanding is context-dependent, i.e. 'situated' (see Lave (1986) on cognition in practice, among many other works).

Ethics from Jenner to Jensen
Thus debates on educational issues and (at the meta level) arguments over how they should be researched have a habit of recurring. Debates on the code of conduct governing research form one perennial example, though (in my view) we have made some moral progress. In 1879, the scientist Edward Jenner borrowed an 8-year-old Gloucestershire schoolboy named James Phipps and infected him with cow pox. Jenner later infected him with small pox. Fortunately, he recovered. This 'scientific' experiment (with a sample of one) led eventually to widespread vaccination. Similar examples have occurred in educational research. In the three examples cited below, one involves unethical *methods*, the second unethical *analysis of data*, and the third unethical *findings*.

We do not have space to explain any of the instances in detail. The first, like Jenner employing unethical methods, was reported by Dennis in 1941. He was involved in the raising of two twins in virtual isolation for a year in order to investigate infant development under conditions of 'minimum social stimulation' (Dennis, 1941). A better known name, Cyril Burt, who is renowned for his testing of 'intelligence' and the assessment of ability has been accused of twisting, manipulating and even fraudulently misrepresenting his data (see Flynn, 1980). Thirdly, the reporting and publicizing of educational research 'findings' has been (and may well be again) accused of being ethically unacceptable. Edward Jensen's notorious study of 'race' and 'intelligence' (Jensen, 1973) concluded that black children had inherently lower intelligence than white children.

Failure to look critically at the fundamental flaws in Jensen's methodology *and* inferences may have led, as Verma and Mallick (1999, p. 39) argue, to subsequent prejudice among many teachers and educators. Similarly, Terman's work (in the same era as Thorndike) 'found' that intelligence was related to social class. As critics, over 40 years later, pointed out (e.g. Karier, 1973) this would be true almost by definition, given the way the IQ tests were constructed, i.e. in terms of the social class order.

These brief notes hardly suffice, but they do show that ethical issues are a common feature in the history of both scientific and educational research.

Changing Approaches to Research
Similarly, approaches and foundation disciplines have changed in the short history of educational research. One of the famous names of the past, and a one-time favourite in teacher training courses, was B. F. Skinner. He did continue the trend of applying psychological research methods to education, but at least some of his research and observation was based in real classrooms as opposed to the laboratory. He is best known (and lambasted) for his initial work on the predictable behaviour of hungry rats, in terms of the stimuli given to them, their responses and the effects of rewarding and 'reinforcing' their behaviour. But his classroom research with children did at least show the importance of positive reinforcement, praise and reward for children's behaviour and learning, a conclusion which has enormous impact for practising teachers.

An equally well-known name in the teacher training courses of the 1960s and subsequent decades has been that of the Swiss researcher Jean Piaget (1896–1980). His research was rooted more in the disciplines of logic and biology than in psychology. Based on relatively small samples (of children, not rats) Piaget developed a model of steps or stages of intellectual development which is still used. Whether this is a theory, a model, an analogy or a metaphor is an issue discussed later. What cannot be doubted is that Piaget's ideas (or models, or theories) have had a major impact on curriculum developments, particularly in the large-scale Science and Mathematics projects of the 1960s and 1970s. They have also had a less tangible impact on classroom teachers, often implicitly, e.g. staffroom discussion of children's 'readiness' to cope with difficult concepts.

Subsequent work by the American Jerome Bruner followed on from Piaget's work and has made an impact on curriculum developments (in Maths and the Humanities) in a similar way. Bruner's belief, based on his research, was that any of the big ideas or key concepts of our inherited body of knowledge could be taught to children in some 'intellectually honest form'. Bruner is also well-known for his concept of 'scaffolding' – a metaphor for the way in which a person's learning can be raised or constructed from a sound base to a new level.

A third name associated with learning and teaching is the Russian Lev Vygotsky. His work, rarely read in its original form, was based on his research into thought, language and social interactions between learners. One of his best known ideas, similar to Bruner's scaffolding, is the concept of a 'zone of proximal development' (ZPD). This is, in some ways, a target zone between a learner's existing knowledge and a potentially new level which he or she can go on to acquire or attain.

The ideas of Piaget, Bruner and Vygotsky are important in considering the history of educational research not only because of their wide applicability but also because it is unclear exactly how their ideas relate to the empirical research carried out by these three famous names. Are the ideas directly derived from their research data by some sort of process of induction? Or do they stem from creative insights, hunches and imaginative thinking? Probably a combination of both, one would suspect. These questions are revisited later when we discuss the meaning and place of 'theory' in educational research.

There are many other valuable ideas in the history of educational research where it is unclear whether they are inferences from the research data, guiding *a priori* hypotheses, imaginative insights or creative models for viewing education. One is Gardner's idea of multiple intelligences (Gardner, 1983) which argues that intelligence has many different facets. Guilford's (1967) model of the intellect, which distinguishes between 'divergent' and 'convergent' thinking, is another example.

The history of educational research is not long, but its ideas (models, theories) have had an impact on educational thinking and educational practice. Influence on the latter is often less tangible and less explicit, however, and its impact is therefore less obvious and often dismissed. The osmosis of ideas takes time. In a sense, we are all 'Freudians' now. In a later chapter we consider recent criticisms of educational research as having no impact on practitioners. My own reading of its brief history is that many of its ideas are taken on board or internalized by teachers or lecturers almost without their notice or acknowledgement. They may be hidden or implicit in staffroom discussions, classroom practice, curriculum development and lesson planning.

The purpose of this brief history, with its limited range of examples, has been to show that none of the major issues discussed in this book are new. The following debates or questions all have a past and will all have a future:

- the relation to, and impact of, research on practice;
- the difference between research in an experimental or a laboratory setting and investigations of naturally occurring situations;
- the range of foundation disciplines which have and have not (and should and should not) relate to educational research: philosophy, biology, history, sociology, psychology;
- the importance of ethics in conducting research;
- the nature and role of theory in educational research.

These issues can all be seen in the changing definitions of educational research which are now presented.

CHANGING (AND RECURRING) DEFINITIONS OF ER

One of the recurring themes in the history of educational research, which surfaces in past attempts to define it, has been the belief that it should attempt to mirror or mimic so-called scientific methods. Thus Gay (1981) defined educational research as: 'The formal systematic application of the *scientific method* to the study of educational problems' (Gay, 1981, p. 6, my emphasis). Nisbet and Entwistle (1970) had earlier commented that educational research should be restricted to 'areas which involve quantitative or scientific methods of investigation'. In the same textbook they argued that the key to educational research is to 'design a situation which will produce relevant evidence to prove or disprove a hypothesis'.

A later definition by Ary *et al.* (1985) follows similar lines: 'When the scientific method is applied to the study of educational problems, educational research is the result.'

These extracts, from only three sources, are sufficient to illustrate three fundamental flaws in attempts to define educational research which were prevalent throughout the last century.

First, there has been a persistent illusion that there is something called 'the scientific method' which 'scientists' follow and which should be adopted by educational research. In the last quarter of the twentieth century there has been a lorry load of publications which show that this belief bears no resemblance to real science (Kuhn,

1970, Medawar, 1979, Woolgar, 1988 are just a few starting points). There is no *one* scientific method; there are as many methods as there are sciences and scientists.

Secondly, it follows that the view of science, and therefore educational research, as being hypothesis-driven has no foundation. Some scientific research may be driven by hypothesis but some is not. Some scientists do experiments and control variables, some do not. Einstein never controlled a variable in his life (discussed in Wellington, 1998).

Finally, one important mistake has been to confuse the terms 'quantitative' and 'scientific', as if the two were synonymous. Quantitative data can (and in my view often *should*) be involved in educational research without thereby inviting the accusation that it is trying to mimic the sciences, or that it is in some way being 'positivist'. Educational research should not attempt to mimic some outmoded view of scientific method, but that does not prevent it from using quantitative data where appropriate. To reject the quantitative while (rightly) denying that educational research should mirror the so-called scientific method would be to throw the baby out with the bath water.

We return to these issues later, but now to some definitions.

It is interesting to note Watson's (1953) comment that

> In education we would do well to stop mimicking the physical sciences. Educational Research is ultimately concerned with people. It is best shared as lay and professional educators are involved.

This is a theme taken up in many later definitions and discussions of educational research, i.e. that research should involve practitioners, not only at the receiving end (as users or consumers) but in the research process itself. The writing of Lawrence Stenhouse is probably the most notable on this theme, with his concept of the 'teacher-as-researcher'.

Stenhouse (1984) defined educational research as

> systematic activity that is directed towards providing knowledge, or adding to the understanding of existing knowledge which is of relevance for improving the effectiveness of education.

We come back to Stenhouse later, but the word 'systematic' is interesting here. In 1986, Best and Kahn defined educational research as

The systematic and *objective* analysis and recording of controlled observations that may lead to the development of generalisations, principles, or theories, resulting in prediction and possibly ultimate control of events. (Best and Kahn, 1986)

Another author to use the word 'systematic' was Mouly, in 1978:

Research is best conceived as the process of arriving at dependable solutions to problems through the planned and systematic collection, analysis, and interpretation of data. It is the most important tool for advancing knowledge, for promoting progress, and for enabling man to relate more effectively to his environment, to accomplish his purposes and to resolve his conflicts. (Mouly, 1978, cited in Cohen and Manion, 1994, p. 40)

Both definitions are notable for their optimism – the beliefs, for example, that educational research might result in the 'ultimate control of events' or that it could enable man (sic) to 'resolve his conflicts'. When we consider the recent criticisms of educational research discussed in the final chapter, this language seems naive rather than optimistic. The term 'objective', used by Best and Kahn (1986), is also extremely problematic. The belief in objectivity in educational research is discussed later.

A fourth source where the word 'systematic' can be found emanates from two of the best known philosophers of education of the later twentieth century. Peters and White (1969) defined educational research as

sustained systematic enquiry designed to provide us with new knowledge which is relevant to initiating people into desirable states of mind involving depth and breadth of understanding.

This definition depends, of course, on their definition of education as initiation into 'desirable states of mind' (or what Peters called elsewhere 'worthwhile activities'), and therefore begs all sorts of questions about what might be desirable or worthwhile, and for whom and where. But Peters and White's main aim was to question the resilient assumption that educational research is just a branch of psychology or social science.

There have been many varied attempts at defining educational research. Themes have recurred and resurfaced. The notion that educational research should be 'scientific' is perhaps the most common, although none of its proponents have attempted to define the word or spell out the meaning of its partner 'scientific method'.

The notion of objectivity has also persisted, again largely undefined. Another theme is that educational research should attempt to generate a body of knowledge and theory. Its alleged failure to achieve this is discussed in the final chapter. Finally, educational research has often been seen, for example, in places in the many editions of the classic text of Cohen and Manion (1980), as the process of producing solutions to problems, i.e. as a problem-solving activity, aiming to provide dependable solutions to the problems of education. Again, seen in this light, it is unlikely to be judged as a success.

ATTEMPTING A DEFINITION

As with most attempts at a watertight definition, those striving to define educational research usually find it much easier to recognize than to define. One of the most widely quoted versions is Stenhouse's (1975) view of research as 'systematic enquiry made public'. Bassey (1990) elaborates on this by defining research as 'systematic, critical and self-critical inquiry which aims to contribute to the advancement of knowledge' (p. 35). The adjective 'critical' implies that the data collected and samples used in the research are closely scrutinized by the researcher. 'Self-critical' implies, similarly, that researchers are critical of their own decisions; the methods they choose to use, their own analysis and interpretation and the presentation of their findings.

In my opinion, this is a sound working description/definition of educational research. It also helps to avoid the perennial and, to me, irritating debate on whether social/educational research is scientific or not. This is not a concern for practising physical scientists who simply 'get on with it', but it seems to have been a 'hang-up' for some social scientists and educational researchers who appear to believe that the addition of the word 'science' (as in 'educational science') confers some sort of accolade or elevated status on their research.

This becomes more ironic when we consider discussions lasting more than 70 years which reveal that physical science is not capable of absolute certainty (Heisenberg, 1958), that the observer in physics is equally as important as the observed (Capra, 1983), that total predictability in a physical system is an impossible goal (see the summary of Chaos Theory by Gleick, 1988) and that most scientific reporting, in fact, falsely portrays science as a clear, logical, linear process (see Medawar's 1963 classic 'Is the scientific paper a fraud?' for the first revelation of scientists' 'cleaning up' of the reality of science research).

It remains a mystery to me why those who work in education should attempt to aspire towards science when scientific methods, processes and codes of conduct at best are unclear and at worst lack the objectivity, certainty, logicality and predictability which are falsely ascribed to them. Surely educational research would do better to aspire to being systematic, credible, verifiable, justifiable, useful, valuable and 'trustworthy' (Lincoln and Guba, 1985).

—2—

Approaches to research in education

There are many different approaches, types or paradigms in educational research, with labels implying opposite poles, such as: positivist/interpretive; interventionist/non-interventionist; experimental/naturalistic; case-study/survey; and qualitative/quantitative. In actual research, however, there may well be a mixture or overlap of the two approaches, e.g. survey and case-study work; collection of qualitative and quantitative data. In addition to these supposed contrasts, we often hear the terms 'action research' and 'practitioner research' used to describe a project or even a paradigm. This section explores briefly some of these terms, but for a full discussion of paradigms and approaches readers will need to dig into some of the many references given at the end of the book.

Interpretive versus Positivist
This is one of the most common contrasts made. Positivists (and I have yet to meet one, even amongst physicists) are said to believe in objective knowledge of an external reality which is rational and independent of the observer. The aim of the positivist researcher is to seek generalizations and 'hard' quantitative data. Positivism is often (wrongly, in my view) perceived as synonymous with 'scientific'.

The concept of positivism is usually traced back to the French philosopher August Comte (with his *Cours de Philosophie Positive*, 1832–42) and the ideas of J. S. Mill (*A System of Logic*, 1843). One of its ideas is that true knowledge is based on the sense-perception of an objective, detached, value-free knower. Positivist knowledge is therefore deemed to be objective, value-free, generalizable and replicable (terms which are discussed later).

The sciences, it is alleged, *do* generate knowledge of this kind, i.e.

objective, value-free and independent of the knower. Thus scientific method is believed to be based on positivist principles.

The positivists in the social sciences and in educational research have argued that sociology, and research in education, should follow the methods of the natural sciences. They therefore advocate a positivist approach. I am not sure whether such people exist any more, at least in the research community. However, as discussed in a later chapter, they may be lurking in the media (see their reporting of educational research), and positivist traits may still linger among certain critics of educational research.

Positivists may be entitled to their opinion but they are certainly wrong on one count. The view that modern science is positivist (even if older science was) is totally false. Modern science cannot always clearly identify and control its variables; it is not always, if ever, successful at determining clear cause–effect relationships, i.e. agent X causes phenomenon Y, and it is rarely objective and value-free. We only have to follow the recent debates on cold fusion, BSE and genetically modified (GM) foods to see this.

The interpretive researcher, however, accepts that the observer makes a difference to the observed and that reality is a human construct. The researcher's aim is to explore perspectives and shared meanings and to develop insights into situations, e.g. schools, class-rooms. Data will generally be qualitative and based on fieldwork, notes and transcripts of conversations/interviews. A crude summary of the two contrasting approaches is shown in Table 2.1 (there is a growing literature on the more specific 'life history' approach within the interpretivist paradigm: two good starting points are Faraday and Plummer (1979) and Sparkes (1994)).

Qualitative and Quantitative Approaches
Unfortunately, the critics of positivism have sometimes succeeded in throwing the baby out with the bath water. As Hammersley (1995) very succinctly puts it:

> We must recognise that absolute certainty is not available about anything, and that attempts to produce absolutely certain knowledge by appeal to serve data, or to serve anything else are doomed to failure. However, accepting this does not mean concluding that any view is likely to be as true as any other, or that anything can be true in some other frameworks if not in ours. (pp. 17–18)

One aspect of the view which Hammersley criticizes is that the

Table 2.1: Contrasting research 'approaches'

	Life history, biography, case study approach	Traditional, positivist approach
Main emphasis	Importance of the observer/author	Detached, 'objective', invisible author; removal of 'the self'
The researcher	Subjectivity acknowledged, researchers put their own 'cards on the table'	Subjectivity denounced, eschewed
Writing	Personal, collaborative writing, account, story	Anonymous, passive tone, impersonal style
Model	Eschews traditional, mechanistic models of the sciences	Attempts to mimic the natural sciences
Aim	Search for 'personal knowledge'	Search for 'objective', generalizable knowledge; separation of 'facts' from 'values'
Researcher's status	Democratic (involves informants and stakeholders), participative, equal status of all	Autocratic – higher status, privilege of researcher

collection and presentation of quantitative data is seen as a positivist tendency and, therefore, not to be pursued. This results from the false polarization of the two approaches in which all the mistaken attributes of positivism are alleged to be present in any quantitative approach. Table 2.2 presents the resulting split between quantitative and qualitative approaches.

Table 2.2 is, of course, a caricature of reality. Quantitative methods are not always theory-laden or hypothesis-driven, and certainly never (because they are employed by people) value-free. Similarly, qualitative research can never be complete fiction; it must depend on some inter-subjective (if not 'objective') reality. The two approaches can complement each other. Background statistics, or just a few figures from available records, can set the scene for an in-depth qualitative study. When it comes to data collection, most methods in educational research will yield both qualitative *and* quantitative data (discussed further in, for example, Layder, 1993, p. 112). Interviews can produce quantitative data; questionnaires can collect qualitative data, e.g. in open response questions; case studies can involve systematic, semi-quantitative observations.

This book is based on the premiss that methods can and should be mixed. To use a simple analogy, if I read a report on a soccer (or cricket, netball or hockey) match, I seek both qualitative (descriptive)

Table 2.2: An exaggerated polarization

Quantitative	Qualitative
Guiding principles	**Guiding principles**
Theory-laden (theory determines practice)	Grounded theory
Hypothetico-deductive	Inductive
Hypothesis testing	Research is descriptive
Replication	'Subjective'
Search for generalization	Value-laden
'Objective'	
Value-free	
Neutral	
Data Collection/Methods	**Data Collection/Methods**
Numerical evidence ('hard data')	Textual evidence (or image-based)
Observations are atemporal, asituational	Researcher is the key instrument, *situated* in the world being studied
Researcher is detached from the situation	
Outcomes are central	Researchers are part of the situation
Social world is like the natural world	Processes of research are central
Data Analysis	**Data Analysis**
Independent of the researcher/analyser	Dependent on the researcher
	Inductive
	Interpretative
View of the World	**View of the World**
Reality is objective	Reality is subjective, constructed
Facts are external	Researcher is central
Researcher is neutral/objective	Reflexivity is vital
Findings are independent of the researcher	
Methods Associated with ...	**Methods Associated with ...**
Questionnaires	Case studies
Surveys	Observation
Experimental (pre-testing, post-testing)	Participant observation
If interviews, structure totally determined by researcher (interviewer totally 'in charge')	Interviews – path and structure partly determined by participants
Sampling	**Sampling**
Probabilistic	Opportunistic
	Purposive

and quantitative (numerical) information. The reporter can wax lyrical about what a great game it was, who played well, how the crowd reacted, who eventually triumphed, and whether the referee survived the ordeal. But I also require the following:

LIVERPOOL   2
(Scorers: Owen, 20 mins;
Fowler, 89 mins)
Attendance: 38,411

ARSENAL   1
(Scorers: Bergkamp, 46 mins;
sent off: Viera, 32 mins)

This may be a crude analogy, but it does demonstrate how qualitative data gives richness and colour; quantitative data provides structure.

Naturalistic Research
Another approach, often aligned with the interpretive, and therefore in contrast to positivism, is often labelled 'naturalistic'. Table 2.3 shows the main features of a naturalistic approach to educational research.

In some ways this is best contrasted with the experimental approach because the former involves research conducted in a natural setting or context as opposed to a controlled, clinical laboratory experiment. In the traditional experimental study a control group is set up with features supposedly identical in all relevant respects (an impossible goal) to an experimental group. Things are done to the experimental group but not the control group, e.g. they are taught with an item of new technology; they use a different teaching or learning approach; as a fictional example (I hope): the experimental group is injected on a daily basis with a wonder drug which makes them learn more efficiently while the control group are given sugar lumps.

Table 2.3: Some features of 'naturalistic' research

1 Setting	Research is carried out in the natural setting or context, e.g. school, home, classroom, playground
2 Primary data gathering instrument	The researcher
3 Background knowledge	Personal, tacit, intuitive knowledge is a valuable addition to other types of knowledge
4 Methods	Qualitative rather than quantitative methods will be used but not exclusively
5 Sampling	Purposive sampling is likely to be preferred over representative or random sampling
6 Design	The research design tends to unfold/emerge as the study progresses and data is collected
7 Theory	Theory tends to emerge from (be grounded in) the data

Source: Lincoln and Guba (1985); Robson (1993)

Practitioner Research
One idea which has received wide recognition in education is the notion of 'practitioner research'. This is research conducted by a practitioner/professional in any field (be they a doctor, a nurse, a policeman, a solicitor or a teacher) into their own practice. Terms and notions expressing a similar idea or research philosophy are 'the reflective practitioner' (Schon, 1983) and 'the teacher as researcher' (Stenhouse, 1975). Practitioner research has a number of advantages, some of which relate to the earlier summary of naturalistic research, e.g. being able to carry out research in a 'natural' setting such as one's own school or classroom. It may also pose certain problems. Table 2.4 sums up the potential benefits and difficulties of practitioner research.

Table 2.4: Practitioner/insider research: potential advantages and problems

Potential advantages	Possible problems
Prior knowledge and experience of the setting/context (insider knowledge)	Preconceptions, prejudices
Improved insight into the situation and people involved	Not as 'open-minded' as an 'outsider' researcher
Easier access	Lack of time (if working inside the organization) and distractions/constraints due to being 'known'
Better personal relationships, e.g. with teachers, pupils	'Prophet in own country' difficulty when reporting or feeding back
Practitioner insight may help with the design, ethics and reporting of the research	Researcher's status in the organization, e.g. a school
Familiarity	Familiarity

Action Research
Another notion linked to practitioner research is the now well-established concept of 'action research'. In one of the classics in this field it was defined as

a form of self-reflective enquiry undertaken by participants (teachers, students or principals for example) in social (including educational) situations in order to improve the rationality and justice of (a) their own social or educational practices (b) their understanding of these practices and (c) the situations and institutions in which these practices are carried out. (Carr and Kemmis, 1986)

This is obviously linked to the idea of practitioner research in that it may well involve a teacher studying, researching into or intervening in his or her own practice, setting or system. But the key aim of action research is to bring about critical awareness, improvement and change in a practice, setting or system. It therefore involves reflection, planning and action as key elements.

There is quite a long history of action research in education dating back to perhaps Lewin (1946) and Corey (1953). Some of the large amount of literature in this area published between then and now is listed at the end of this book. Each discussion seems to attempt its own diagram to show the process of action research, and many are, in my view, far too complicated to be of real value. The essence of the process seems to be a spiral of cycles involving

PLANNING – ACTING – OBSERVING/EVALUATING – REFLECTING – RE-PLANNING

and so on. My own attempt to present this as a diagram is shown in Figure 2.1.

Research students sometimes ask the question: 'Is what I'm doing "Action Research"?' The answer probably lies most clearly in the *intention behind* the research. If the research is conducted with a view to *changing* or improving a situation, e.g. a policy, a curriculum, a management system, then it probably merits the label of action research. But for some advocates of action research this description would probably be too broad and would include too much. A less inclusive definition would be to say that action research involves intervening in a situation and later evaluating that intervention. This would be part of a cycle:

identify the issue or problem → research it → suggest action → implement action → evaluate → revisit the issue/problem

Research of a contrasting kind (though it would be derogatory to call it 'non-action' research) would have the purpose of studying, exploring or illuminating a situation – it might not be driven by the intention to change it. Such research would therefore not intervene in the situation (except that every researcher or observer has an effect on the situation being studied), and would probably not manufacture or create a situation, i.e. it would explore events or situations occurring naturally. (One of the best summaries of the ideas of action research

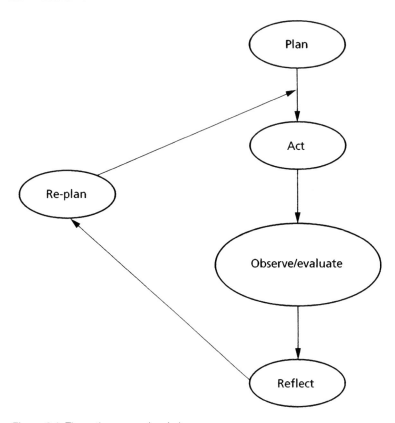

Figure 2.1: The action research spiral

was written by a teacher who carried out her own action research project based in Bath: see McNiff, 1992.)

METHODS AND METHODOLOGY

Methodology?

Methodology is defined by the *Shorter Oxford English Dictionary* as the 'science of method' or, more historically, as 'treatise on method'. My own interpretation of methodology is: the activity or business of choosing, reflecting upon, evaluating and justifying the methods you use. Indeed, the latter is an essential feature of any written report or research thesis, i.e. justifying the decisions we have made on methods. No one can assess or judge the value of a piece of research without knowing its methodology. Thus, the aim of methodology is 'to describe and analyse methods, throwing light on their limitations and resources, clarifying their suppositions and consequences, relating their potentialities to the twilight zone at the frontiers of knowledge' (Kaplan, 1973). The research process itself therefore involves a scrutiny or an evaluation of methods: 'the methods we choose are there to be tested, just as much as the substantive hypothesis' (Walker, R., 1985a).

Although most of this book discusses methods, often in a very practical vein, it should not be forgotten that methodology, i.e. reflection on those methods, is a vital part of any research project, small or large.

Box 2.1 summarizes some of the key aspects of methodology in educational research.

Box 2.1: Methodology

... thinking about methods, reflecting on them, evaluating them, assessing your data ...

- Why did you use them?
- What was the quality of the data they gave you?
- Can you learn lessons, or perhaps 'generalize' from the data?
- How could your sample have been better?
- Could, or should, other methods have been used? Why?
- How did you (the researcher) affect the data you collected?

Mixing Methods: Triangulation

Even in a small-scale study, a mixture of methods can often be adopted. Schatzman and Strauss (1973) refer to such an approach as 'methodological pragmatism':

> The field researcher[1] is a methodological pragmatist. He sees any method of inquiry as a system of strategies and operations designed – at any time – for getting answers to certain questions about events which interest him.

Such a view therefore implies that qualitative and quantitative methods can exist side by side in an enquiry: 'there is no fundamental clash between the purposes and capacities of qualitative and quantitative methods or data' (Glaser and Strauss, 1967, p. 17).

The concept of using a multi-method approach in collecting data,

---

[1]Most commentators on the choice of method in carrying out an empirical study in social science use terms such as the field, field research, and field researcher (e.g. Burgess, 1984 and 1985a; Fettermen, 1984). These terms will be followed here.

information or evidence (these terms are discussed on page 83) is discussed in full by Cohen and Manion (1994) in the chapter entitled Triangulation. They discuss types of triangulation and their advantages. They define triangulation as 'the use of two or more methods of data collection in the study of some aspect of human behaviour' (p. 254). The origin of the term lies in the use by navigators, surveyors, military strategists or others involved in physical measurement, of several locational markers to pinpoint a certain position or objective. In research, triangular techniques can be used to 'map out, or explain more fully, the richness and complexity of human behaviour by studying it from more than one standpoint and in so doing by making use of both quantitative and qualitative data' (*Ibid.*, p. 233).

A typology of triangulation has been suggested by Denzin (1970) who lists the principal types of triangulation which might be used in research. The types can be summarized, briefly, as follows:

1. **Data triangulation** which is subdivided into:
   (a) time triangulation: the researcher attempts to consider the influence of time using cross-sectional and longitudinal research designs;
   (b) space triangulation: researchers engage in some form of comparative study, e.g. of different regions, different countries;
   (c) person triangulation at the following levels of analysis:
       (i) the individual level;
       (ii) the interactive level among groups;
       (iii) the collective level.
2. **Investigator triangulation**: more than one person examines the same situation.
3. **Theory triangulation**: alternative or competing theories are used in any one situation.
4. **Methodological triangulation**, which involves 'within method' triangulation, that is the same method used on different occasions, and 'between method' triangulation, when different methods are used in relation to the same object of study.

(after Denzin, 1970)

This book relates mainly to research involving methodological triangulation of the latter kind, i.e. where a variety of methods are used to study the same issue. However, another important kind of triangulation can be used when analysing and reporting on individuals' views and attitudes gleaned from surveys. Triangulation can be achieved by checking with the individuals that your interpretation matches, and accurately reflects, their views and attitudes.

THE PLACE OF 'THEORY' IN ER

> There is nothing so practical as a good theory. (Lewin, 1946, p. 169)

One of the perennial debates in educational research over the years has concerned the status, the purpose and the function of theory. The matter is complicated, of course, by lack of agreement over what educational theory *is*. The issue is complex but it is an important one for anyone involved in educational research. The discussion of 'theory' is more than a theoretical matter – students, writers and researchers are often accused of lacking a theoretical framework or a 'theory base' to their work.

Practical outcomes of this accusation could be the non-award of a higher degree by thesis, the rejection by a referee of an article submitted for publication or the refusal of a funding body to hand over thousands of pounds. In short, being accused of lacking a theoretical base or, even worse, of being 'a-theoretical' can be, practically, very serious.

What Is 'Theory'?

Like most problematic words, 'theory' does not lend itself to easy definition – and, worse, we cannot (unlike the proverbial undefinable elephant) always recognize one when we see one. The *Oxford English Dictionary* shows that the word originates from the ancient Greek idea of a 'theor', a person who acts as a spectator or an envoy, perhaps sent on behalf of a state to consult an oracle. More recently, the word theory was taken to mean a mental view or a conception; or a system of ideas used or explanation of a group of facts or phenomena (dated 1638 in the *Oxford English Dictionary*).

In the physical sciences, the distinction between phenomena/events (i.e. things which happen), laws and theories is relatively clear. A *law* is a statement telling us *what* happens in terms of a general pattern or rule. If a metal rod is heated it expands; if pressure is exerted on a gas in a container, its volume decreases (Boyle's Law); every action has an equal and opposite reaction (Newton's Third Law). Laws are simply statements of patterns or connections. For this reason they are less tentative and more long-lasting than theories. I would wager my entire life-savings that the law 'When a gas is heated it expands' (Charles' Law) will be true in two centuries from now. But the theories used to encompass or support laws are more tentative.

Theories are used to explain *why* specific events and patterns of events occur as they do. As such, they are explanations constructed by human beings, and therefore subject to improvement, refinement and sometimes rejection, i.e. they are tentative.

Take a concrete example: if some air is trapped in a tin can and heated, its pressure increases. This event or phenomenon is one instance of a general law which says that 'Gases trapped in a container and heated will increase in pressure' (the Pressure Law). But *why* does this happen? The current theory (the Particle Theory of Matter) tells us that everything (including a gas) is made up of tiny little bits, called particles, which jiggle around all the time, get faster and faster when heated and bang against the wall of their container harder and harder. This theory is good enough to explain why heating gases makes them expand if they are allowed to, or just increases their pressure if they are trapped. It is just a theory, but it is a very good one, and has its roots in the time of Democritus a couple of millennia ago.

But Democritus' idea that matter is made up of tiny, indivisible particles, like billiard balls, is just not good enough to explain other events and phenomena, e.g. electricity or radioactivity. These phenomena required new theories at the end of the nineteenth century and the beginning of the last. The atomic model of that era portrayed Democritus' 'atmos' as being 'rather like' the solar system with a nucleus in the middle and electrons orbiting round the outside. This model, or theory, lasted well, and still works in explaining many events. But it has since been superseded by the quantum theory of matter and the introduction of new subatomic particles, such as quarks and leptons, to explain new, observed phenomena. Similarly, the theories of Newton, which work perfectly well in everyday life, have been complemented by Einstein's Theory of Relativity, which is broader and capable of explaining at a more 'universal' level.

So what has this to do with educational research? First, theories are used to explain *why* things happen. They *are* tentative, but not that tentative (Newton was born over 300 years ago and his theories still have widespread applicability and practical value, e.g. building bridges; getting to the moon and back). Secondly, theories are a way of *seeing things*. They often involve models, or metaphors, which help us to visualize or understand events, e.g. the atom is 'rather like' the solar system. Thirdly, the existence of an established theory (certainly in science but more debatably in educational research) can shape or determine the way we subsequently 'see' things. In short, observation in science is often *theory-laden*. The theory determines the observation. In the context of educational research we return to this debate later – does theory determine observation and data-collection, or does theory 'emerge' from our observations or data?

Finally, it needs to be noted that an established theory can *predict* as well as explain, i.e. theories may be predictive as well as explanatory. The particle theory of matter can be used not only to explain what happens to matter, e.g. phenomena like melting or boiling, but also what *will* happen in new situations, e.g. if impurities are added, how will boiling be affected? Similarly, the theory that the Earth's surface is rather like a jigsaw puzzle or a collection of plates (the theory of plate tectonics) can be used to explain not only why earthquakes occur but also to predict future occurrences.

Theories in Educational Research

The role of theory in educational research, just like the physical sciences, is to help us to understand events and to see them in a new or a different way. A theory may be a metaphor, a model or a framework for understanding or making sense of things which happen in education. Other elements in educational research which are sometimes (often unjustifiably) given the name 'theory' are little more than generalizations, alleged patterns, ideas or even mere labels.

My own view is that a theory in educational research is only worthy of the name if it helps us to *explain* phenomena, and thereby aid our understanding of it. It provides a new way of 'seeing' things. A theory may also have *predictive* power as well as explanatory value, although this may be expecting too much in educational research. Metaphors and models often fulfil at least the first criterion. To take examples from learning theory, we can see Vygotsky's idea of a 'zone of proximal development' and Bruner's notion of 'scaffolding' as useful metaphors. Metaphors are like bridges (the word metaphor literally means 'carry over' or 'carry across') which link the unknown or the unfamiliar to the known or familiar.

Models are similar in that they provide highly simplified representations of very complex events or realities. A classic case is the world-renowned map of the London Underground: a simplification or idealization of a messy, complicated system. But the model or map we use serves its purpose. Similarly, models of teaching, education or the learning process are simplifications of reality. But, like metaphors, they help in making complex situations clearer, more intelligible and, therefore, better understood. Piaget's model of stages of development is one example: it is a simplification of reality, especially if taken too literally (and wrongly) as a series of discrete, concrete steps with definite ages attached to them. But it has great value in explaining conceptual progress and children's development, especially when it is related to curriculum demands (see for example, Shayer and Adey, 1981, and subsequent work by Adey). My guess is that many teachers apply Piaget's ideas unwittingly in their own practice and staffroom discussion.

One final point in ending this sub-section concerns the use of *labels* which have emerged in educational research. For example, Shulman (1987) has identified and labelled different categories of 'teacher knowledge' which teachers draw upon in their practical teaching. These are often labelled (though Shulman's actual categorization is more refined) as 'subject knowledge' (SK) and 'pedagogical content knowledge' (PCK). The latter includes teachers' knowledge of explaining, putting things across, pedagogy, breaking down complex ideas into simpler steps, and so on. Generally, it relates to the art, craft and wisdom of teaching. Shulman's ideas have great application in considering initial teacher education, mentoring, professional development and other areas. But are they theories? My own view is that they do help us to understand the above areas, and underlying the labels are valuable conceptualizations or categorizations. They have some explanatory value and, perhaps, even predictive power. A similar discussion could be held over Schon's idea of the 'reflective practitioner' (Schon, 1983), Willis' notion of 'the lads' (see Appendix 1), the label 'vocationalism' (applied by many authors to the growing links between schooling and industry/employment in the 1980s), or the notion of the 'hidden curriculum'. Perhaps in the end it is a semantic debate over whether they are theories or not.

When Does Theory Come in: a priori or a posteriori?

The key question for those engaged in, or about to embark on, educational research is not *whether* theory should make its entry but *when*. One of the recent criticisms of educational research (Chapter 12) is that new research is not always based on previous work, i.e. it is 'non-cumulative'. It is argued that, in turn, this has led to the failure of educational research to create a sound, reliable body of knowledge which can inform practitioners and ultimately improve education (as, allegedly, medical research has done with medical practice).

Whether or not these criticisms are justified is discussed later. The point here is: how can educational research become 'cumulative'? Should theory be brought in prior to the research in order to guide it and make observation theory-laden, i.e. *a priori*? Or should theory 'emerge' from data collection and observation and be developed from it, i.e. inductively, *a posteriori*?

On the one hand, Anderson (1990) urges that 'in your study and prior knowledge you should attempt to identify appropriate theoretical and conceptual frameworks which bare [sic] relation to your problem' (p. 47). He counsels researchers to ground their research in antecedent work which has 'generated contemporary constructs guiding subsequent investigation', i.e. data collection will be theory-guided or theory-laden to use the term from science.

An apparently opposite approach is to generate theory (inductively) from the data. Theory 'emerges' as the data collection progresses and is firmly 'grounded' in it, and derived from it, i.e. *a posteriori*. This approach is often called 'grounded theory' (after Glaser and Strauss, 1967).

So the crucial questions are: Should categories, patterns or theories be generated from the data, or should they be imposed upon it? How can research be 'cumulative' if it does not use previously determined categories? Do researchers have to recreate theory every time they collect and analyse data?

These are complex and important questions. But the simple answer is that it depends on the nature of the research, its purpose and the area being investigated. In some fields there are ample theories, sufficiently well developed, and it would be wrong not to use them in shaping research design and data collection. In others there may be a shortage of suitable theory, or it may be extremely tentative, thus implying a different approach. Similarly, with the purpose of a research project, a key aim of a project may be to *replicate* previous research in order to lend support to a theory, or perhaps to attempt to refine it. In others, the aim may be to develop new, tentative theories which, perhaps, subsequent researchers might build upon.

These are all issues which we return to later in considering research approaches, 'paradigms', methodology and methods.

TWO CONTENTIOUS TERMS: VALIDITY AND RELIABILITY

These are two terms which have been widely used in discussing research, not least educational research. They also tend to be abused, partly because they are difficult to define and to understand. For example, the terms are often, especially in conversation, used to signal approval. Thus people may say, in meetings, for example: 'That's a valid point', meaning no more than that they agree with it. Similarly, people (including the media) may describe a piece of research as 'reliable', meaning that they approve of it and/or trust the person or team who conducted it. The two words do have technical meanings, however, and I will attempt to define them and also to give a loose intuitive meaning for them here.

Validity
Validity refers to the degree to which a method, a test or a research tool actually measures what it is supposed to measure. For example, in the old debate on IQ tests the main issue was whether the tests actually did measure what they claimed to measure, i.e. intelligence. Does our ability to do an IQ test measure our intelligence, or does it simply measure our ability to do an IQ test?

There are three important points here which apply across the whole of education and educational research.

First, we can never be 100 per cent sure of validity. We can only lay some sort of claim that our test or method is valid. The only claim that we can make with certainty is the circular or tautologous one that, for example, a person's ability to do a test, whether it be of numeracy, literacy, intelligence or spatial awareness, measures their ability to do that test on that day at that time under those conditions. Hence the issue of reliability.

Secondly, any discussion of validity rests squarely on the foundation of how the characteristic being measured is *defined*. Thus 'intelligence' may be defined in a certain way and this may then increase the validity of something which sets out to measure it. We could even complete the circle the other way by defining intelligence as: 'the ability to succeed in an IQ test'. It would then follow that those tests will have 100 per cent validity. However, this would seem a somewhat vacuous way to proceed. But if we treat 'intelligence' as a highly problematic term (e.g. by adopting the model that people have a range of intelligent abilities or 'multiple intelligences') then a traditional IQ test becomes invalid. In other words, any assessment of validity depends heavily on the definition or meaning of the term underlying it, and many of these terms in education are extremely problematic: understanding, ability, achievement, numeracy, literacy, learning, development, knowledge, IT literacy, and so on.

Finally, there is an essentially insoluble problem of internal validity in research and in all our knowledge generally. We can only know reality by observing it or measuring it; and how can we know that our measurement or observation corresponds to reality?

There is no higher court of appeal to which we can turn. We only have our perceptions – the only way we can judge whether our perceptions match reality is to appeal to our perceptions. We are caught in a circular trap – the only saving grace is that we are all caught in the *same* trap. Hence the importance of sharing, communication, inter-subjectivity and mutual control.

The problem of external validity is no more soluble – this is an assessment of the degree to which our observations or measurements can be generalized from, i.e. extended to other 'external' groups or domains which have *not* been observed or measured.

Le Compte and Preissle (1984) explain this clearly, although their use of the word 'scientific' is unnecessary:

> Distinctions are commonly drawn between internal and external validity. Internal validity is the extent to which scientific observations and measurements are authentic representations of some reality. External validity is the degree to which such representations may be compared legitimately across groups. (p. 323)

We can never claim to be sure of either. To do so would be to commit what the philosopher David Hume called the 'fallacy of induction'.

Reliability

The term 'reliability' is equally contentious. This is a judgement of the extent to which a test, a method or a tool gives consistent results across a range of settings, and if used by a range of researchers. It is linked to the idea of 'replicability', i.e. the extent to which a piece of research can be copied or replicated in order to give the same results in a different context with different researchers.

Le Compte and Preissle (1984, p. 332) define reliability and claim that no researcher studying the social world can achieve total reliability. They describe it as

> the extent to which studies can be replicated. It assumes that a researcher using the same methods can obtain the same results as those of a prior study. This poses an impossible task for any researcher studying naturalistic behaviour or unique phenomena.

I would concur with this view – but the consolation is that current philosophers and sociologists of science are increasingly sceptical about the possibility of total reliability and replicability in modern scientific research (see, for example, Collins, 1985 and Woolgar, 1988 as early examples of this scepticism).

As for an intuitive 'feel' for reliability and validity, the best analogy I know is the situation in which a group of people attempt to measure the depth of an empty swimming-pool with an elastic, stretchy tape measure. They do not realize that the swimming-pool has a deep end and a shallow end. They each take measurements at different points along the pool believing that this is the average depth, so their measurements are invalid (they are not measuring what they think they are measuring). In addition, some measurers stretch the measuring tape more than others – the elasticated ruler is unreliable. The researchers are unreliable in that they cannot all be relied upon to hold the ruler at exactly the same tension (understandably).

A FEW CAUTIONARY NOTES

Some of the more general problems inherent in any study of human organizations and societal patterns were discussed at length by Schon (1971), and are worth considering in this context before embarking on a discussion of method. In a chapter entitled, aptly, 'What can we know about social change?', Schon pointed to four problems 'inherent in public learning': gaining knowledge, the status of data, designing an experiment and extrapolating from results.

Schon argues that one of the problems in gaining knowledge of social change is that 'data gathering is a political process' (p. 207). This raises problems of access (in Schon's example, of his entry into a black neighbourhood) and of the perceptions of those doing research.

The second problem is that 'data may not endure' – and may become out-of-date almost as soon as it is collected. Schon goes on to discuss the problem of diagnosing and interpreting data. People will interpret data differently according to their own personal perspective.

The next problem in 'public learning', as Schon calls it, is the great difficulty of designing any scientific or even systematic experiment in studying society: 'it is almost never possible to hold some variables constant while manipulating others' (*Ibid.*).

Finally, Schon points to the fourth main difficulty in studying social change: the problem of extrapolating or generalizing from the results of any study. This is linked to the problems inherent both in gathering data and interpreting it. A number of perspectives will be involved in a given study, making data collection, interpretation and therefore extrapolation, problematic.

Schon's discussion of problems in public learning draws examples mainly from areas of public planning and policy, but his conclusions are relevant to the attempt to gather data in the fields of education and training (i.e. the difficulties of access, perception and datedness in gathering data; the problem of interpretation; the impossibility of designing an 'experiment'; and the danger of extrapolation). These inherent difficulties are all taken as starting points for the discussion that follows.

—3————————————————————

Research literature

————————————————————

Before discussing particular methods in Part 2, it is worth reminding ourselves that we need to find out what is already 'known' in our area of research, what's been done before and, just as important, how it's been done. This is an aspect of research which many of us, including physical scientists at times, are apt to neglect.

The main general rule is that any study should be located in the context of what has been done before. Your job is not just to mould your own brick but to slot it into the wall of existing understanding in that field.

READING AND REVIEWING THE LITERATURE IN A CHOSEN AREA

Choosing a topic for research and then 'focusing down' an inquiry in that area is a difficult task. The next task is equally difficult: exploring the literature available in that area.

Knowing where and when to *stop* is a far more difficult problem than knowing where to start. In some fields it is best to start from a seminal or much-cited paper and go from there – a method which can be called 'snowball searching' (c.f. snowball sampling). Each paper will have references at the end which will lead to other references, and so on. The problem is that the process is rather like a chain reaction and the list of publications one 'should' read grows exponentially.

The growth is multiplied when one begins to use the wide range of bibliographies, indexes and lists which are now available, many of them electronically. Table 3.1 gives a list of some of the main sources which can be of value in ER. Some are accessible via the Internet, some on CD-ROM, others on microfiche, with some still available in paper and print.

Table 3.1: Ten sets of sources for educational research

1. Bibliographies
British National Bibliography (BNB)	lists all British publications
British Library OPAC	the on-line catalogue for the British Library
National Union Catalogue	American equivalent of BNB
Library of Congress OPAC	American equivalent of the British Library OPAC
British Books in Print (BBIP)	lists books under author and title
Books in Print	American equivalent of BBIP

2. Periodical indexes and abstracts
ASSIA (Applied Social Sciences Index and Abstracts)	covers the whole area of the social services
British Education Index	indexes the contents of c.300 UK journals
Current Index to Journals in Education (ERIC)	American equivalent of the British Education Index
Social Sciences Citation Index	bibliographic database with citations
Sociology of Education Abstracts	covers books as well as journal articles

3. Report literature
Resources in Education (ERIC)	an important source of report literature
British National Bibliography for Literature	official and semi-official documents from LEAs, university departments and other agencies concerned with education

4. Research in progress
Register of Educational Research in the UK	lists all the major research projects
Current Research in Britain	details of research in British universities

5. Theses and dissertations
Index to theses	references to UK theses
Dissertation abstracts	references to US and European dissertations and theses

6. British government publications
Census for 1981 and 1991	
UKOP (United Kingdom Official Publications)	covers all British official government publications and important international ones

7. Statistics
Annual Abstract of Statistics
Education and Training Statistics for the United Kingdom
Resources of Higher Education Institutions
Social Trends
Students in Higher Education Institutions
UN Statistical Yearbook
UNESCO Statistical Yearbook

8. Conference proceedings
Index of Conference Proceedings
(produced by the British Library)

9. Newspapers
Daily Telegraph/Sunday Telegraph
Guardian
Independent/Independent on Sunday
Observer
Times/Sunday Times
Times Educational Supplement
Times Higher Educational Supplement
Times Index

10. Networked information services
The NISS (National Information Services and Systems) Information Gateway Service
offers access to a range of international information sources relevant to UK
universities, e.g. subject-specific Internet resources, bibliographic services, news,
reference sources and information about higher education and IT.

Source and acknowledgement: Denise Harrison, University of Sheffield Library (see
also Harrison, 1999)

The ultimate aim of using electronic networks is usually to find
and obtain literature which is available in printed form, i.e. on paper.
However, an increasing number of sources, e.g. journal articles, are
available electronically, and some may *only* be available electronically. A useful guide on referring to and citing on-line sources was
provided by Li and Crane (1993).

It is clear from Table 3.1 that there is a wide range of sources for
educational research, many of them accessible using information and
communication technology (ICT), i.e. via the Internet or CD-ROM.
ICT can be of enormous value in exploring the literature but its
power is in some ways a double-edged sword. Searching with ICT
will yield a huge number of references. Careful searching techniques
using carefully chosen key words, and logical operators such as AND
or NOT, can narrow down the shoal of references hauled in by a
literature trawl. But even with a fine-mesh net the use of ICT applied
to the sources in Table 3.1 will produce a large catch. It then depends
on the hard work and discretion of the researcher to make the task of
reviewing the literature manageable.

One other valuable source is people. Researchers at all levels can
sometimes use people who may be experts in the field. If you cannot
arrange to see them, write, telephone or e-mail them asking for help
and advice. It is surprising how willing are experts in a field to give

up time and energy to someone who is, or will be, working in the same field.

Only the researcher can decide which references to follow up, which ones to skim or which to examine closely, and which publications to 'weave into' the eventual thesis, article or book. The process has to stop somewhere. But the lines and boundaries can only be drawn by the researcher, and the drawing of these lines has to be justified in writing up.

JUDGING OTHER PEOPLE'S RESEARCH

One of the difficulties of reviewing the literature is knowing when to stop and where to draw the boundaries. An equally difficult skill is to be able to judge – critically but fairly – the research reported by others. We tread on dangerous ground if we examine too negatively the work of others – ancient slogans about not throwing stones if we live in glasshouses spring to mind. But there are certain areas, and within them certain criteria, which can be applied when examining research reports critically. I suggest ten, though there are probably more:

1. *The Title*: Is it descriptive, i.e. does it accurately reflect what is in the article? Is it attractive? (see Woods, 1999, p. 28: the title should be 'informative', 'accurate', 'succinct and clear', 'designed to awaken interest').

2. *The Abstract*: Does it tell you why the research was done and why it's important; how it was done, with whom, with what, and what were the key findings? Does it provide a map for the reader?

3. *The Literature Review*: Does it give an overview of the range of literature related to the research? Is it new or creative in suggesting other, alternative areas of literature which might be 'laterally applied' to this area? Does it explain where and why boundaries were drawn?

4. *Theoretical Framework*: Does it start from a theoretical framework which might help to inform it or structure it? Does it shed light on any existing theories or models? Does it lead (inductively) to new theories or models?

5. *The Aims of the Research*: Is it addressing a significant problem or issue? Are its aims and purposes clear? Is it reasonably well-focused?

6. *Methodology*: Do the methods chosen match the purposes/aims?

Why were these methods chosen and not others? Did they prove to be appropriate and productive?

7. *Sampling*: On what grounds was the sample chosen, e.g. why these schools/colleges; why these classes? Why these documents or reports?

8. *Evaluation, self-evaluation and reflexivity*: Is the research evaluated, both for 'content' and method/methodology, i.e. is it a reflective account? Do the researchers evaluate their own role, their own position and their effects on what is being researched, i.e. are positionality and reflexivity included?

9. *Drawing out conclusions and implications*: Have the data been 'milked' for all they are worth? Are the conclusions related back to the literature review – are the two woven together? Do the researchers stick their necks out too far . . . or not far enough?

10. *Presentation*: Is it clearly written and well-structured? Is it turgid and verbose? Could Ockham's razor have been applied in places? Does it have at least some storyline?

To observe all of these ten points is difficult; they are counselling perfection. But they can be useful in examining literature for a review. Perhaps the main criterion is that a research report should be reasonably transparent or open. This is one of the useful points made by Tooley and Darby (1998) in a critique of educational research that was not warmly received.

> One of the criteria of good practice in educational research should be to be told enough information about the research conducted to enable informed judgements to be made about its conduct and reporting of results, or to allow it to be, where appropriate, replicated and tested. (p. 46)

PRACTICAL TIPS

First, always make notes on what you are reading. This will help you to read actively with your own research in mind and keep you engaged. Keep full bibliographical notes (especially dates and page numbers) as you go along – this will save a huge amount of checking and searching at the end. Failing to keep detailed references to useful ideas or valuable quotes and then spending days later searching for them is one of the cardinal sins I am always committing. Keeping a card index for references suits many people, others use a software package such as 'Endnote', while it can be done simply by keeping an alphabetical list on a separate disk or file.

Finally, try to organize and categorize the literature you read as you go along. Themes or categories can be coded, again using either a card index, a sub-divided, word-processed list or a software package. Knowing these categories, and deciding which ones are central and which are marginal, can be invaluable in deciding where to stop with a literature review. It can also be a great help when writing up (see Chapter 12).

BOOKS ON RESEARCH METHODS

There are a large number of books about educational research and 'how to do it'. One of the best known and widely recommended over a long period for postgraduate (and some undergraduate courses) is Cohen and Manion, now in its fifth edition (2000). This is a large book, rather like Robson (1993), which seems to cover almost every-thing anyone would want to know. Both are essential for the book-shelf but neither are suitable for reading cover-to-cover. They have also been accused of presenting research in a prescriptive, unprob-lematic, recipe-like fashion. Walford (1991), for example, writes of books of this kind:

> These books and others like them present research largely as an unproblematic process concerned with sampling, questionnaire design, interview procedures, response rates, observation and so on. They present an idealised conception of how social and educational research is designed and executed, where research is carefully planned in advance, predetermined methods and procedures followed and 'results' are the inevitable conclusion. (p. 1)

Here I think he is being rather unfair on recent books, and his critique certainly would not apply to Robson (1993). But the value in Walford's point comes later when he first accuses educational research of trying 'to justify its own procedures by making them as "scientific" and "objective" as possible, and by aping what may have been perceived to be the methods of the natural sciences'. The problem then arises that when the new researcher inevitably 'finds unforeseen difficulties, conflicts and ambiguities in doing research, he or she will tend to see these as personal deficiencies arising from insufficient preparation, knowledge or experience' (Walford, 1991, p. 2).

One solution is to have the 'research methods textbooks' on the shelf but also to read actual accounts of research which people have done. Some of these have been mentioned above, and are deemed 'classics'. This also includes books outside the obvious field of 'education' such as William Foote Whyte's (1943) prewar study of a 'street corner society' and Holdaway's (1985) insider view of the police force.

My own list of 'classics' from education, which I recommend to people for providing an insight into some of the research of the last 30 years, is given in Appendix 1. Some are well known and widely cited – others I have chosen for providing valuable examples of interesting case study work, interesting methods or interesting reporting and discussion.

In addition there are a few valuable collections of semi-autobiographical accounts which researchers have written about their own experiences – the good bits and the bad bits. Two of the best are Burgess (1984), with ten case studies, and Walford (1991), with ten more accounts of what really happened in some of the best known studies of the last 20 years.

The researcher's role and responsibility

THE RESEARCHER AND THE RESEARCHED

In social and educational research the researcher himself, or herself, is the key 'instrument'. This is now generally accepted, even if it was contested in the earlier history of educational research. Even in the biological and physical sciences it is now (at last) more widely accepted that the researcher plays a key role. Thus, Medawar (1963) talked of the 'myth of objectivity' in the sciences. Polanyi (1967) talked of the importance of 'mutual control' among scientists in regulating their work, i.e. inter-subjectivity rather than objectivity (my words). The physicist Heisenberg had, 40 years earlier, developed his Uncertainty Principle, which stated (roughly) that we cannot determine the exact position *and* momentum of a particle. This, effectively, brought to an end a belief in a Mechanistic, Predictable, Deterministic Universe – subsequent developments such as Chaos Theory put further nails in the coffin. At the atomic or sub-atomic level the measuring instrument seriously affects or disturbs what is being measured. The Researcher affects the Researched. A similar rule applies in educational research; a rule we might call the 'Education Uncertainty Principle': the researcher influences, disturbs and affects what is being researched in the natural world, just as the physicist does in the physical universe.

Minimizing the Researcher Effect

One option might be to ignore this effect or perhaps to attempt to diminish it. The latter has been done in examples of 'covert research'. Hockey (1991), for example, in his research on 'squaddies', spent a lengthy period with young soldiers in training-camps and on the streets of Northern Ireland. He was able to pass as one of them due to his previous experience as a soldier. Similarly, Holdaway (1985) spent four years 'inside' the police force, and researched their practices while working as a policeman. Fielding (1981) took an even more risky role as a member of the National Front while carrying out research into the behaviour of its members.

These are all examples of covert research (discussed more fully in the section on ethics and also by Scott and Usher, 1999, pp. 129–30). Less extreme and less deceptive strategies have been adopted by researchers who attempt to become accepted by a group, but who do not deceive them totally. This has been done by dressing in a similar manner or behaving in a similar way to the group in order to gain acceptance and establish a rapport. Such an approach might be part of ethnography, which is discussed later.

Reflecting on the Researcher Effect: Reflexivity and Reflectivity
An alternative is to acknowledge the effect of the researcher, accept the impossibility of a neutral stance and to bury finally the myth of the 'neutral observer'. In Wolcott's (1995, p. 186) terms, every researcher has a healthy bias:

> I regard bias as entry-level theorising, a thought-about position from which the researcher as inquirer feels drawn to an issue or problem and seeks to construct a firmer basis in both knowledge and understanding.

Reflecting on this bias is part of the business of reflexivity.

Being 'refl*ex*ive' is part of a more general approach to research – being 'refl*ec*tive'. The former is a sub-set of the latter.

Being reflective involves thinking critically about the research process; how it was done and why, and how it could have been improved. Reflection is an important part at every stage, i.e. in formulating questions, deciding on methods, thinking about sampling, deciding on presentation and so on. Most writers on research (in education and the sciences) would agree on its importance and many would argue that these reflections and evaluations should be put into print in reporting the research and going public.

But an important part, or subset, of 'reflectivity' is the notion of 'reflexivity'. This involves reflecting on the self, the researcher, the person who did it, the me or the I.

The 'x' in the word reflexivity denotes the self, the person who did the research, the subject. In Hammersley and Atkinson's terms (1983, p. 234), reflexivity requires 'explicit recognition of the fact that the social researcher, and the research act itself, are part and parcel of the social world under investigation'. Another author (Bonnett, 1993, p. 165) has referred to it as 'auto-critique'.

Thus being ref<u>lex</u>ive is an important part of being ref<u>lec</u>tive, but they are not the same thing.

The extent to which reflexive accounts should be included in writing up and publishing research is open to debate. Thus Hammersley and Atkinson (1983) argue that it 'is no good being reflexive in the course of planning and executing a piece of research if one is only to abandon that reflexivity when it comes to writing about it?' (p. 209). Similarly, Stephen Ball has argued that it is a 'requirement for methodological rigour that every ethnography be accompanied by a research biography, that is a reflexive account of the conduct of the research' (Ball, 1990, p. 170).

But how much of this auto-critique or self-analysis should educational researchers engage in … or indulge in? Troyna (1994) was highly sceptical of the 'confessional tone' of many research biographies which have become almost obligatory in educational research. He accused some authors of suffering from 'delusions of grandeur'. More seriously, he argued that excessive use of reflexivity or research biography could diminish the status of qualitative research in the eyes of its critics in populist circles such as the newspapers and other media (see page 4).

My own view is that reflectivity and the more specific reflexivity are vital (but different) parts of the research process and should not be confused. Reflection is part of evaluation and forms an important component of any research, including in the sciences. Being reflexive is equally important but does not merit an excessively long, confessional, autobiographic account which includes unnecessary details. A statement of the researcher's position ('positionality', as it is often called) can be brief and should include *relevant* information only. Personal information such as gender or age may be important for readers of the research, but other details (such as shoe size, to take a silly example) are not. Ockham's razor should be applied.

Questioning and Exploring Positions
One of the roles of any researcher in education is to examine and question the positions or assumptions which are often taken for granted:

1. The first task, as discussed above, is to question any assumptions about yourself: your own values, ideas, knowledge, motivation and prejudices. For example, What's my own position in relation

to this research? What are my relevant past experiences and prior knowledge? Am I carrying a bias, a prejudice, or insider information which will affect my role as researcher?

2. The second task is to examine the assumptions taken for granted by institutions, such as schools, colleges or employers. What are their sub-cultures and underlying values? Does the rhetoric of their public documents or mission statements, e.g. in a brochure or prospectus, match the hidden values, ideas, ethos and assumptions? An outsider may sometimes be better placed to question and examine these than an insider (see discussions on ethnography). Similarly, the assumptions and tacit ideas or values in one institution can often be exposed and challenged by comparing it with another.

3. Finally, the researcher's role is to examine and question the *language* used in discussing education. This might be the *spoken* language of teachers, lecturers or policy-makers during interviews (or in an ethnography, overheard conversations); or it might be the *written* language of documents such as White Papers, prospectuses, curriculum legislation or minutes of meetings. Both the style or tone and the actual words need to be questioned – for example, the hackneyed terms and buzz words of the 1990s. Words and terms which spring to mind are 'effective teaching', 'good practice', 'delivery', 'continuity and progression', 'equality', 'standards', 'failing schools', 'school effectiveness'. Who uses them? Why? How are they used? Does everyone have the same understanding of them? For a researcher, whose work includes some documentary analysis, when did they come into our written language and where from?

The role of the researcher, as (I think) Sara Delamont first said, is to 'make the familiar strange'.

THE ETHNOGRAPHIC APPROACH

The activity of 'ethnography' is a branch of anthropology, which is (roughly speaking) the extended study of human societies, institutions and social relationships by getting 'inside them'. It is now widely discussed in educational research, though my own (sceptical) view is that few alleged examples of ethnography in research on education are genuine instances of anthropology. Many involve an ethnographic approach but few genuinely merit the label of 'an ethnography'.

The key research strategy employed in ethnography is participant observation. The researcher enters the social world of persons and groups being studied in an attempt to understand their shared meanings and taken-for-granted assumptions. There are varying degrees of participation, from total immersion (when the researcher is a full participant who is also an observer) to a more marginal position when the researcher is no more than an observer who occasionally participates (this spectrum of approaches to observation is discussed more fully on pages 93–4).

There are two main issues in examining ethnography:

1. Since ethnography depends on the researcher becoming (to a greater or lesser extent) an insider, the 'observer effect' on the people or setting being studied is more important than in any other approach. The researcher's questions, body language, dress, observations, comments and indeed their very presence in a social situation will have an impact. The researcher needs to reflect upon this impact and carefully consider his or her influence on the setting and the people in it, e.g. a school and its staff (see discussion on reflexivity).

2. A second key issue is the business of gaining access and entry. This has been particularly important in ethnographies of football hooligans, street corner gangs, fascist organizations such as the National Front, the mentally ill and the police force (see, for example, Goffman, 1961; Whyte, 1943; Holdaway, 1985 or Fielding, 1981). In some of these studies, which in my view were genuine ethnographies, the researcher's own safety was put at considerable risk. This is unlikely (though not impossible) in educational research. The strategy in the above examples was to go in 'under cover', and to maintain this cover at all costs (see Bulmer, 1982, on covert observation). But covert research of this kind, apart from its ethical difficulties, presents enormous practical problems in educational research. An adult researcher may be able to pass as a new member of a teaching or lecturing staff, and gradually become accepted and therefore party to insider knowledge, insights and conversations. But the researcher's role is to probe people's views, prejudices and taken-for-granted assumptions – this will mean asking apparently naive questions, and often some fairly awkward ones, which will automatically set the researcher apart.

The situation is magnified if an adult researcher attempts an ethnography with pupils or with students. To what extent can he or she become one of them, without being seen as 'patronizing'? Should the researcher attempt to dress as they do, behave as they do and even try to speak with the same accent, using the same language? Such an approach is likely to be met at best with suspicion, but more likely derision. One tactic has been to employ collaborators, e.g. pupils or students to collect data on their own peer group (Farrell *et al.*, 1988, did this with American high-school students). But this is not always practical and may be ethically questionable, e.g. by putting the students collaborators at risk.

My own view is that there have been few genuine ethnographies in educational research (for a range of examples to consider critically see Ball, 1981; Spindler, 1982; Burgess, 1983; Hargreaves, 1967; Lacey, 1970 and Willis, 1977). The present climate in education makes the ethnographies of the 1960s, 1970s and 1980s increasingly difficult to carry out. Despite this there are many important features in the ethnographic approach (for example, in interviewing, observation or making extensive field notes) which are valuable in educational research. These are discussed at various points in this book.

PLANNING AND DESIGNING RESEARCH

Research Process and Research Design
The research process has often been depicted as a linear, logical sequence starting with the formulation of aims, then planning, collecting, analysing and interpreting data, and ending with conclusions and writing up.

One example of the 'ideal' research sequence is shown in Figure 4.1. This is based on a seven-step sequence proposed by Howard and Sharp (1983) and is reproduced by Gill and Johnson (1997) in an excellent book on managing research. They rightly suggest that each of the seven steps be given equal attention, with particular emphasis on clearly defining the research topic. This structure is useful as a checklist for planning or as a reminder but in reality the process in educational research is far more messy than this.

As Medawar (1963) famously pointed out, this after-the-event portrayal is a fraud, and many others since have admitted that it does not happen like this. Medawar often called research a mixture of 'guesswork and checkwork'. A realistic approach (see Figure 4.2) is to admit that the process is cyclical in that people go back and replan/refocus their research, collect and analyse their data and realize that they need more, or different, data; start to write up and realize they are addressing the wrong questions; find that the targets or samples

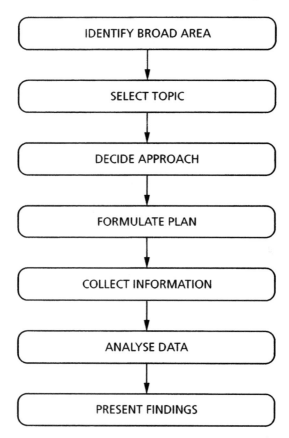

Figure 4.1: The ideal model of research

they have set themselves are too low/high, and so on. Even the cyclical version in Figure 4.2 is a cleaned up and idealized version of what really happens. I suppose the only certain thing is that, eventually, the research has to stop and the report or thesis has to be sent to print, though having heard stories of PhDs lasting 20 years or more, the endpoint for some research cycles might be death!

Clarifying the Purposes of Educational Research
The starting point for a research project may be a question, or questions, that you would like to address. It may be an idea or a hypothesis you wish to test. A slightly less focused start might be an issue to be explored or, more ambitiously, a problem to be solved.

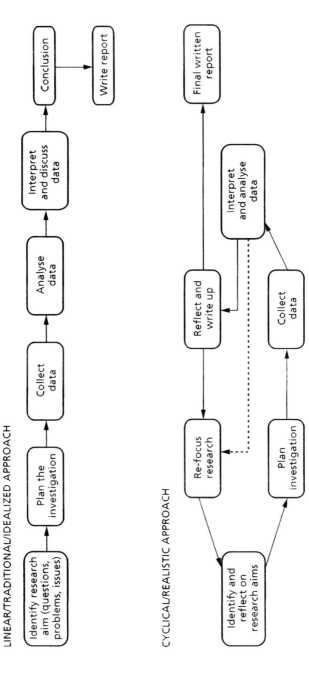

Figure 4.2: Linear and cyclical research plans

These four possibilities can 'help to define the immediate purpose of a research inquiry' (Bassey, 1990).

Stating or formulating your purposes under one (or perhaps more) of these categories can help at all stages of a research enquiry, especially at the outset, i.e.

- What question(s) are you asking/addressing?
- What hypothesis are you testing?
- What issue(s) are you exploring?
- What problem(s) are you trying to solve/alleviate?

If you can formulate the questions you wish to ask, it then helps to decide whether they are

- 'what, which or where' questions;
- 'how' questions; or
- 'why' questions.

'What, which or where' questions often involve descriptive research, sometimes a fairly straightforward collection of information. For example, What computer programs are most commonly used in Y5 of primary education? Which children in a certain school have parents who participate in the daily reading scheme? Where are the multi-media stations in secondary schools located? These kind of questions might form the aim of a research project, i.e. simply finding out the names, numbers or extent of something; or they might lead on to more exploratory or explanatory research, i.e. finding out how a scheme or programme is working or is being used, or why teachers/ parents/students behave in certain ways or use certain methods/ resources more than others.

The 'why and how' questions (i.e. exploratory and explanatory) are usually the more interesting but invariably the most complex and intractable.

Horses for Courses: Matching Methods to Questions

Framing research questions should always be the first step in the research process. It should always be a case of *questions first, methods later*. For example, it makes no sense to decide: 'I am going to use questionnaires/interviews/observations' before clarifying the questions which you wish to address or shed light upon. As discussed earlier, they may be what, which, where, how or why questions. The former may imply a straightforward collection of information, perhaps a survey approach. But the latter, i.e. the how and why questions which seek *explanations* will demand more in-depth exploratory approaches, e.g. a detailed case study.

Methods and methodology are discussed more fully throughout this book. For this introductory section, I simply suggest (for the early, planning stages of research) a 'horses for courses' matrix. This is shown in Table 4.1.

Table 4.1: A questions-methods matrix (horses for courses)

Research methods → Research questions ↓	Questionnaire	Interview	Observation	Follow-up interviews	Document analysis	etc. . . .

Once the research questions have been formulated down the left of the matrix, the appropriate methods can be decided upon along the right. Some research questions might demand several methods, others only one. These are decisions which need to be made in the planning stages, but, given the complexity of educational research, will need to be reviewed and revised in the light of other difficult decisions, e.g. gaining access (see later).

A fuller discussion of this aspect of research planning can be found in Denscombe (1998, pp. 3–5). He summarizes it well by writing:

> good social research is a matter of 'horses for courses', when approaches are selected because they are appropriate for specific aspects of investigation and specific kinds of problems. They are chosen as 'fit for purpose'. The crucial thing for good research is that the choices are reasonable and that they are made explicit as part of any research report.

We return to this last point in the chapter on writing.

Difficult Decisions for the Researcher
Another way of portraying what really happens in educational research is shown in Figure 4.3. This shows the difficult decisions

that have to be made in real research. They cannot always be made in the ideal order. For example, we may plan to interview a certain sample of people, e.g. teachers, students, only to find that we cannot gain access to them, e.g. they are unwilling, too busy, too sensitive or just fed up with 'being researched'. This may, in turn, force us back to re-consider our methods and even our original research questions. All the decisions are intertwined and connected by arrows going both ways. Even constraints on the way the research must be presented, e.g. in the form of a book or thesis which is written *and* in the public domain, can impinge upon decisions about who to involve in the research and which methods to use.

A rather messy Figure 4.3 is an attempt to represent the difficult and inter-connected decisions which go into the *actual* design of an educational research project, as opposed to the idealized version.

Managing and Organizing Research

Educational research is a messy business and it would be wrong to pretend otherwise in a report, article, thesis or a book. One of the most common activities in real research is *compromise*. We compromise over time spent, distance travelled, methods used, samples chosen, literature reviewed, words written and money spent. This is partly because it involves people rather than, as Michael Polanyi (1967, p. 32) once put it, 'cobblestones': 'Persons and problems are felt to be more profound, because we expect them yet to reveal themselves in unexpected ways in the future, while cobblestones evoke no such expectations.'

But there are certain steps, guidelines or just handy tips that can be followed in planning, organizing and conducting research:

1. The first 'exhortation' (because many preach it but fewer practice it) is: Keep a research diary from the very beginning. The contents and length of a diary are partly a personal matter but it could include:
   - a chronological record of what was done, where, when, etc., e.g. events observed, people interviewed, names to contact for gaining access;
   - a record of observations, field notes etc;
   - notes of methods and methodology;
   - questions, ideas, hunches, memos;
   - categories, patterns or themes beginning to emerge.
   One of the best early articles on keeping a research diary is Burgess (1981).

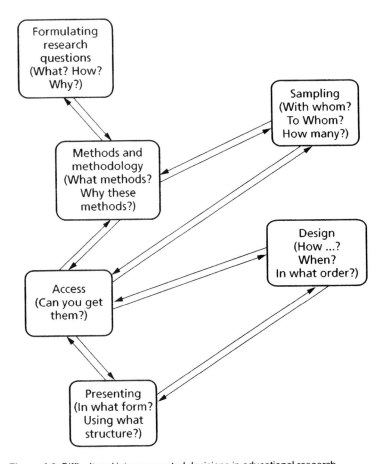

Figure 4.3: Difficult and inter-connected decisions in educational research

2. 'Squirrelling': start writing and recording – and collecting other material such as documents – from day one. I use the cardboard box method in which all relevant material is gathered in a box, eventually leading to separate boxes (or files) for each chapter (for a book) or section (for an article). Some people (myself included) like to use a separate disk for each chapter. Gradually, the material builds up, either in paper or electronic form.

3. Planning and devising a timetable: it is worth making a realistic timetable for the different stages of research even if you do not, or cannot, keep to it. As discussed earlier, advance plans on paper bear little resemblance to final reality, but they are still worth making. Setting short-term, achievable goals is worthwhile. Be

prepared to revise your plans, given the 'people not cobblestones' warning of Polanyi.

4. Making contacts and gaining access: this is a vital job in the early stages which we discuss later. It is worth noting (in the diary) the key people whose permission is needed, e.g. headteachers, principals, parents, even governors. It is essential to follow *correct protocol*, for ethical as well as practical reasons. This may involve telephone, e-mail and sometimes formal letter-writing. The purpose, procedures and eventual outcomes of the research will all need to be made transparent to all those involved, not least young people.

A lot more could be, and has been, said about planning and organizing research but my intention has been to be brief. An amusing list of research tips, which can be useful as a checklist throughout a research project, was suggested over twenty years ago (Wilson, 1980). An adapted and updated version of this is shown in Box 4.1.

Box 4.1: 39 steps (but not in this order) for MA, MEd, MPhil, PhD, EdD students

1. Don't panic too often.
2. Be nice to librarians (especially in inter-library loans).
3. Remember that your supervisor . . .
4. Find out how *you* work best.
5. Always have a couple of areas you can work on at any time.
6. Read a few theses in your area, at your level.
7. Plan ahead.
8. Don't think that photocopying is the same as reading.
9. Keep your writing structured.
10. Put your external's book on the bibliography.
11. Don't think it will be absolutely perfect . . .
12. . . . read your supervisor's thesis.
13. Remember that ideas change in three years – what you wrote at the outset may need changing.
14. Write *your* introduction first: write the reader's last.
15. Don't be afraid to point to your strengths and to the weaknesses of others.
16. Keep *full* bibliographical details.
17. Have someone to comment on your writing style at an early stage.
18. Set yourself short-term goals . . .
19. . . . and if you aren't meeting them, work out why.
20. Allow *plenty* of time for writing up.
21. Step back from time to time.
22. With each piece of work ask if it is worth doing.

23. Don't begrudge *some* time spent on reading very widely.
24. Find out early on about length, presentation conventions and submission dates.
25. Talk to people about it.
26. Don't begrudge time spent on thinking.
27. Keep writing.
28. Don't think that reading just one more book will solve all your problems . . .
29. . . . and don't use that as an excuse for not starting writing.
30. Criticize, evaluate, analyse; don't just describe.
31. Buy a book on punctuation.
32. Use your research to make contacts.
33. Using quotations doesn't make the idea any more true . . .
34. . . . and you can usually write it better yourself.
35. Use a card index or a disk for references, ideas etc.
36. Don't be afraid to be imaginative.
37. Make sure your bibliography is comprehensive.
38. If you set something aside for a while, make some notes about your ideas for its continuation.
39. Organize an efficient filing system.

Source: Adapted and updated from Wilson's 50 research tips, in Wilson (1980) 'Group sessions'. *British Journal of Guidance and Counselling*, **8**(2), 237–41.

ETHICS: THE RESEARCHER'S RESPONSIBILITIES

Ethics in Educational Research

Ethics and morals play an important part both in educational and scientific research. Ethics are important in the physical sciences (which investigate inanimate objects) but figure even more prominently in the biological sciences where plants and animals are the objects of study. This factor is multiplied in educational research, where people are studying people.

Morals underpin ethics, but the two terms are not quite synonymous. An 'ethic' is a moral principle or a code of conduct which actually governs what people do. It is concerned with the way people act or behave. The term 'ethics' usually refers to the moral principles, guiding conduct, which are held by a group or even a profession (though there is no logical reason why individuals should not have their own ethical code).

My own view is that the MAIN CRITERION for educational research is that it should be ethical. Hence it is worth not only devoting some space to it here but, more importantly, for every researcher to place it foremost in the planning, conduct and presentation of his/her research. Ethical considerations override all others.

Box 4.2 (based on my own experiences) gives some concrete

examples of the moral dilemmas and ethical questions that a researcher may well encounter.

Box 4.2: Ethical problems? A few specific examples and questions

1. A pupil being interviewed tells you that X is a 'crap teacher' and hates his lessons because 'they're boring'; or a pupil gives you important but highly personal information about her home life, e.g. abuse.
2. A teacher passes on a secret, a piece of confidential information about the school or a colleague or a pupil.
3. During an interview, a teacher comments unfavourably on an individual student or on a colleague's teaching ability (what do you do about gossip generally?); or a teacher makes a racist comment.
4. Teachers/pupils/students want to know what you have found out about
   a) fellow pupils or teachers or lecturers;
   b) the school, college etc.
5. Items of relevant information are picked up accidentally, and unbeknown to the informant, e.g. in a toilet, a corridor or a staff room.
6. You observe a classroom through a glazed, but closed, door, or from round the corner, or a small adjoining room.
7. When does formal observation/interviewing end and informal observation/casual conversation begin?
8. Can a viewpoint/piece of information given in confidence be used in a research report?
9. In writing up, how can you give the relevant details of context, e.g. size of school, region, gender/age of an informant, without compromising confidentiality/anonymity?

I will not go through each example in turn but by considering such situations I have used them to produce my own set of rules, or code of conduct, which is shown later. But first, a few general issues.

An educational research project could be unethical in five ways:

1. The *design* or planning of the research might be unethical, e.g. by using an experimental and a control group and unethically treating or mistreating one. Even the formulation and phrasing of the research *questions* could be ethically unacceptable, e.g. why does X achieve more than Y?
2. The *methods* employed might be ethically unacceptable. This could include the business of gaining access (discussed later) or the actual conduct of the research.
3. The *analysis* (or manipulation) of the data might break ethical rules, e.g. ignoring certain results or observations (as the Greek astronomer Ptolemy did), or selectively filtering out qualitative data from interview transcripts if it does not 'fit' your hypothesis.
4. The *presentation* or reporting of the research could be unethical or

disrespectful, e.g. revealing names or portraying a group of young people as foul-mouthed yobs.

5. The *'findings'*, conclusions or recommendations of the research might be unethical (for an example from history see Jensen, 1973).

Thus educational research might be unethical in its design, its methods, its data analysis, its presentation or its conclusions (incidentally, research in the sciences could equally well be unethical in any of these five areas, despite the myth that it is value-free).

Codes of Conduct and 'Responsibility'

There have been many discussions of the ethical issues facing researchers in education. A valuable collection in the late 1980s was edited by Burgess (1989). Three years later, the British Educational Research Association published a set of Ethical Guidelines on research (BERA, 1992). One of its main themes was that of 'responsibility', which in turn implies certain rights and rules. A few of the numbered paragraphs are selected below to give a flavour of this valuable document. One paragraph talks about gaining not only the consent of all the participants in a study but also their 'informed consent':

7. Participants in a research study have the right to be informed about the aims, purposes and likely publication of findings involved in the research and of potential consequences for participants, and to give their informed consent before participating in research.

The importance of seeking permission from the right people, through the right channels is also stressed:

8. Care should be taken when interviewing children and students up to school leaving age; permission should be obtained from the school and, if they so suggest, the parents.

The list could be extended to include other 'gatekeepers': in addition to headteachers (or principals) and parents, research may require the consent of the head of a local authority, a council leader, a union leader or (if studying, say, employers' views on education) a managing director or personnel head.

Perhaps the overriding rule is that honesty and openness should prevail:

9. Honesty and openness should characterize the relationship

between researchers, participants and institutional represen-
tatives.

The BERA guidelines are valuable in that they highlight the
responsibilities of a researcher. Responsibilities in educational
research fall in several areas: responsibilities to the participants, to
the teaching or lecturing profession, to the research community and
(in funded research) to the sponsoring body or council. This range of
responsibilities, especially in funded research which may be driven
and pressurized by an outside body, may sometimes be difficult to
reconcile and balance. My own view is that there is no room for
'moral relativism' in doing educational research, i.e. there are certain
rules which should not be broken. The area of ethics (unlike, in the
views of some, methodology) can never be a domain where 'anything goes' (Feyerabend, 1993). For this reason I have put forward
my own set of guidelines in Table 4.2 which I feel should not be
broken.

Table 4.2: Watch your ethics: eight rules to follow

1. No parties should be involved without their prior knowledge or permission and informed consent, i.e. they know what they are letting themselves in for and where your 'findings' *might* be publicized.

2. No attempt should be made to *force* people to do anything unsafe, or do something unwillingly, e.g. have their voice tape-recorded.

3. Relevant information about the nature and purpose of the research should always be given.

4. No attempt should be made to deceive the participants.

5. Avoid invading participants' privacy or taking too much of their time.

6. Benefits should not be withheld from some participants (e.g. in a control group) or disadvantages imposed upon others (e.g. in a control or experimental group).

7. All participants should be treated fairly, with consideration, with respect and with honesty.

8. Confidentiality and anonymity should be maintained at every stage, especially in publication.

THE KEY: SENSITIVITY AND RESPECT

See Robson, 1993, pp. 30–5 for further discussion.

If researchers work in a team they should devise a set of ethical
principles which they all agree upon and adhere to.

SAMPLING: CHOICE AND COMPROMISE FOR THE RESEARCHER

Samples and Populations

A sample is a small part of anything which is intended to stand for, or represent, the whole. Thus we can smell a sample of perfume, drink a sample from a glass of wine or sample a small piece of fudge before we buy the whole bar. In these everyday examples we have faith or trust in the belief that the perfume, the sip of wine or the tiny square of fudge either smells or tastes like the whole thing. In educational research, the business of sampling is not quite so straightforward. For good, practical reasons we have to select a sample from the whole range of possibilities, i.e. the entire *population*, as it is called. With the sip of wine we can be fairly sure that it *represents* the entire bottle, i.e. the whole 'population'. However, we could not safely extrapolate that the sip represents *all* bottles of wine of the same make and same year.

The same applies to educational research: when we choose a sample (which we must), e.g. a class of Year 8 children, how can we be sure that our sample represents the entire population, e.g. every Year 8 pupil in the UK? Moreover, can we extrapolate to every pupil of that age band in Europe, or to the northern hemisphere, or to the world?, i.e. deciding on what counts as the 'population' we are sampling from is often just as problematic as the sampling itself.

The simple answer is that we can *never* be sure that our sample is fully representative of the whole population, wherever we draw the lines. Sampling always involves a *compromise*. This is equally true of so-called statistical, quantitative research. One of the beliefs underlying this approach is that by taking a sample at random from an entire 'population', it may serve to represent the whole. But we can never be absolutely sure that a random sample (unless it forms 100 per cent of the population, which is, in practice, impossible) is representative. We can only estimate a certain probability that the part represents the whole. Thus anyone who holds the view that quantitative research using random samples *can* be generalized from, and that qualitative research cannot, is completely mistaken. Every kind of research needs to be assessed and evaluated as to its generalizability.

Probability and Non-Probability Sampling

Probability and non-probability sampling can be distinguished. The former group of methods (which involves random sampling, systematic sampling and stratified sampling) is perhaps more suited to the large volume, postal survey.

Non-probability sampling is perhaps more feasible and more informative in qualitative research for a number of reasons. First, due to the intensive nature of fieldwork, convenience sampling on a non-probability basis may be the only option open to a project or an individual. This may also help to overcome the problem of access or gaining entry. This problem, so commonly raised in discussions of ethnography (see, for example, Hammersley and Atkinson (1983); Woods (1986, pp. 22–32)), can often be eased by convenience sampling rather than attempting an apparently more rigorous, probability sample. For example, personal contacts and links may already exist with a school, college or employer that can be usefully exploited to gain quality information, rather than attempting to forge new links or gain new entry for the sake of a probability sample.

Non-probability sampling also includes purposive sampling and snowball sampling (Cohen and Manion, 1994). Both can be valuable in following up contacts, checking data from similar organizations, and generally exploring the field. Purposive sampling, as its name implies, involves using or making a contact with a specific purpose in mind. 'Snowball' sampling, in a sense, follows from this, although it may not always be purposive, e.g. it may be involved with the problem of gaining access if, for example, one interviewee suggests another willing and valuable contact worth following up.

An important type of non-probability sampling is a major feature of ethnography and is often referred to as theoretical sampling (after Glaser and Strauss, 1967). Glaser and Strauss were primarily concerned with the generation of theory from research which is, in their sense, 'grounded'. This notion, though somewhat difficult to interpret, implies that theory is somehow generated and emerges from the research itself. This emerging theory then, in turn, dictates the process of data collection and sampling: 'The process of data collection is controlled by emerging theory' (p. 45).

Such a developing process need not conflict with early decisions on sampling, e.g. probability sampling, which may have been non-theoretical. Initial decisions on data collection can be based upon a general perspective on a problem rather than a 'preconceived theoretical framework' (Glaser and Strauss, p. 45), but as the research develops (and grounded theory with it) sampling will become more theoretical. This point is emphasized in a later discussion of method by Hammersley and Atkinson (1983) who

Table 4.3: Probability and non-probability sampling

Probability	Non-probability
Definition: a sampling plan in which it is possible to specify the probability that any person, school, college or other unit on which the research is based will be included in the sample.	*Definition*: a sampling plan where it is not possible to state the probability of a unit being included in the sample.
Examples: • random sampling • systematic sampling, e.g. every tenth person; every fortieth school • stratified random sampling, i.e. random selection within groups or strata of a population	*Examples:* • purposive/judgement sampling (choice of sample serves the purposes/ objectives of the investigation) • convenience sampling • snowball sampling (members of one sample lead to others . . . and so on) • practicality sampling ('the art of the possible') • theoretical sampling (sampling guided by emerging theory) • quota sampling (sampling made up of quotas in different categories, e.g. class, age, ability etc.)
Advantages • allows a statistical generalization to any population beyond the sample surveyed • attempts to eliminate the judgement or bias of the researcher	*Advantages* • valuable for a pilot survey • probability sampling is often impossible to achieve • likelihood of higher response rate • usually the only option in small-scale research

suggested that sampling should be 'intentional, systematic and theoretically guided'. Lincoln and Guba (1985) called it 'emergent and sequential' (p. 92).

Table 4.3 gives a summary of different types of probability and non-probability sampling. It should be pointed out that judgement and probability sampling may sometimes be combined, e.g. a school or other unit may be selected for its convenience or its special features and then random samples of, say, pupils or classes may be taken within it.

Sampling is therefore of vital importance in both qualitative and quantitative research. In the former, the samples are unlikely to be 'statistical' or 'probabilistic' samples, i.e. samples which can be believed to represent the entire population from which they are taken. This in turn presents one of the difficulties over 'generalizability'. In other words, the business of sampling, generalizability and access (all discussed later) are completely interwoven.

In qualitative research it is vitally important to reflect carefully on sampling; and later, in any form of publication (e.g. a written report), to be able to justify, honestly and openly, the sampling procedure followed.

Types of 'Purposive' Sampling

It is worth taking time now to summarize the various sampling strategies that could be used in qualitative research. They can all be given the general label of purposive or purposeful sampling. Several strategies have already been discussed. Some additional possibilities, with reference to fuller discussions are:

- *maximum variation sampling*, in which the researcher explores some phenomenon by seeking out people, settings or organizations which represent the greatest differences or extremes of that phenomenon (discussed, for example, in Patton, 1990; Taylor and Bogdan, 1984; Lincoln and Guba, 1985).
- *typical* case sampling will involve selecting cases, e.g. people, students, schools, colleges, which are *believed* to be fairly typical. On the contrary, a researcher might choose atypical or very extreme cases in order to understand some phenomenon because such cases are believed to be particularly illuminating.
- *critical* case, or special case sampling: this involves selecting carefully chosen cases (e.g. pupils, students, organizations) with certain special characteristics, e.g. so-called 'gifted' children, schools deemed to be particularly 'effective', or a college reputedly offering 'good practice' in a certain area (e.g. its provision of key skills to all students). Indeed, schools, colleges or employers exhibiting 'good practice' in a certain field are often chosen for case-study sites for evaluations (discussed later), especially if the aim is to study 'good practice', analyse it and disseminate its key features to a wider audience.

There are a range of sampling strategies with different labels, many of which overlap, e.g. criteria sampling is virtually the same as critical case sampling. A summary of various possibilities, with possible examples, is shown in Table 4.4, some of which apply in both qualitative *and* quantitative educational research.

How do we select from this range in educational research? It depends on a range of factors including time, resources and access –

Table 4.4: Some types of 'purposive' sampling

Label	Summary	Example
Maximum variation	Deliberately selecting a wide range of different cases	A group of teachers/lecturers with varying ages, experience, background or qualifications
Opportunistic	Opportunities or cases present themselves during fieldwork	Chance encounters with a teacher/employer/former colleague
Convenience	Accessible, easy-to-contact, well-known (to you) people or settings	Colleagues in a school/college/company
Typical	Persons or organizations believed to be normal or 'typical'	A 'typical' comprehensive school
Atypical	Cases clearly outside the norm	A certain type of student; an 'exceptional' school
Criterion	A more generic label for samples chosen according to predetermined criteria	All the pupils in a school who have been excluded
Snowball	One case suggests another who suggests another ... (also called 'ancestry' or 'recommendation' sampling)	One employer recommends another with an active interest in education and training
Critical	Choosing special cases for certain purposes	Colleges who are reputed for 'good practice' in a certain field
Guided (directed) sampling	An informant, a knowledgeable guide or an expert directs the researcher to people or settings, and may help with access	An 'expert' in a field suggests particular settings, e.g. schools/colleges, or people, e.g. teachers

but most importantly it depends on the purpose of the research. Maykut and Morehouse (1994, p. 56) summarize it succinctly:

> the selection of a sampling strategy depends upon the focus of inquiry and the researcher's judgement as to which approach will yield the clearest understanding of the phenomenon under study.

Incidentally, they take the view that increased understanding is the main purpose of qualitative research and therefore 'the goal of a qualitative study is not generalisability' (*Ibid.*, p. 57). This issue is discussed more fully later.

GAINING ACCESS

The Problem of Access

Whatever plans we might make in educational research, they are almost certain to be compromised – or in some cases completely scuppered – by the problem of gaining access to what we want. This might involve access to people, to places, to organizations or to documents (a further practical difficulty is often one of gaining access to, getting hold of, the articles and books which are the necessary reading in preparing for a research project).

In this section we will only consider access to people and organizations or institutions (a later section in the book looks at access issues in documentary research). Start with some extreme examples: in the UK many of us would like to interview the Prime Minister and a range of his minions in the Education Department; some researchers might like to interview a range of 'captains of industry' to ascertain their views on education and training; one might like to interview a range of convicted criminals in high-security prisons to probe their educational backgrounds; someone might even wish to interview or observe the President of the United States.

In every one of these extreme cases, access is likely to be impossible and would therefore force the unrealistic researcher to return to their drawing-board. But there are far less fantastic examples where access may well be a problem; for example, interviewing all the pupils who have been excluded from a given school in, say, the last three years; interviewing all the headteachers from a cluster of schools; observing the lectures, or the lessons, of every lecturer, or teacher, in a given department; interviewing a random sample of parents and/or observing them at home helping their children.

In all conceivable cases, unrestricted access and a 100 per cent success rate are likely to be difficult if not impossible to achieve, often for purely practical reasons (and sometimes for ethical or safety reasons).

The business of access can therefore seriously affect the design, planning, sampling and carrying out of educational research. Educational research is always the art of the practical or the 'art of the possible' (Medawar, 1979). But we have to do something, and a compromise is always involved. This is why opportunistic or convenience sampling (discussed elsewhere) feature so commonly in educational research (which, by definition, involves access to people).

Guidelines in Gaining Access
Access is difficult; it requires time, effort and perseverance. But there are certain guidelines which can be followed in improving it. These may help to avoid upsetting people, 'getting their backs up' and falling foul of any of the ethical issues discussed elsewhere.

1. First, remember that a researcher may be viewed in a selection of different ways by a school, a college, an employer, a parent, a teacher, etc.: as an academic whose feet are 'off the ground', as a suspicious stranger, as a knight to the rescue, as a friend or confidante, as a trusted colleague, as an education expert, or as a puppet or instrument of the head, the principal or the managing director. Attitudes towards the researcher are likely to vary from suspicion, mistrust or cynicism, to awe, trust or friendship. It is to be hoped that any negative viewpoints and attitudes at the outset would give way to positive attitudes and dispositions towards the end of the research.
2. Secondly, the important first task is to establish individual contacts who can act as a link, i.e. names with direct phone numbers or e-mail addresses. These 'contact points' will help with the next task which is to ascertain which people, or gatekeepers (Becker, 1970), and channels need to be gone through in order to gain permission and consent. This involves understanding the structure and hierarchies in an organization, e.g. a school, a college or an employer. Insider knowledge needs to be tapped in order to follow the correct protocol and to not leave anyone out (especially those who might take offence).
3. This links to the next task which is to make clear to all concerned the extent of the study, the demands it will make, the reasons for doing it and the likely forms of publication. This will involve telling people exactly what will be expected of them (e.g. a 30-minute interview, being a member of a focus group, filling in a two-page questionnaire) and telling them what you plan to do with it. This applies as fully to pupils, students or apprentices as it does to teachers or lecturers.
4. Fourthly, the researcher needs to become aware, as early as possible, of any sensitive or controversial issues which might arise – for an individual or for an organization. As mentioned in the first point, subjects of research may feel threatened or intimi-

dated by a newcomer – a researcher or even by an insider adopting the role of researcher.

5. Finally, and less seriously, whenever you visit a new building, organization or institution, always expect that somebody there is not expecting you! It may be the receptionist, the secretary or the caretaker, the headteacher or the principal – but my wager is that at least one person will say: 'we weren't expecting you today', or show their surprise in a similar way.

These are just a few of the points needing consideration in gaining access. They are partly a matter of common sense and (as quoted elsewhere) a good general approach is to establish yourself as a credible person doing a 'worthy project' (Woods, 1986, p. 23). Dress and behaviour will also be important in gaining access. Numerous commentators on ethnographic research have stressed the importance of dress and manner in 'getting in' (Delamont, 1992; Hammersley and Atkinson, 1983). No less important is the problem of establishing rapport and credibility in interviewing.

A final concern in gaining access is to establish contact with a key informant, i.e. someone who can provide the information required either to maintain a sampling strategy or to allow the development of theoretical sampling.

The important general point is that it would be foolish to pretend that a project could be designed and planned, or sampling established, before access had actually been arranged; hence the portrayal of 'messy decisions' shown earlier (Figure 4.3) and the unrealistic idea that a research project proceeds along a straightforward linear pathway.

Access by Stealth? Covert and Overt Approaches in Educational Research
There are some who argue that access should be gained covertly. The principle behind this idea is the justifiable belief that the subjects of the research will not behave 'naturally' if they know they are part of a research study. This applies, of course, largely to observation studies and has been called 'covert participant observation'. Bulmer (1982, p. 4), for example, describes the situation as one in which

> the researcher spends an extended period of time in a particular research setting concealing the fact that he is a researcher and pretending to play some other role. In such a situation, the identity of the researcher and knowledge of his work are kept from those who are being studied, who have no knowledge that they are being studied.

The purpose is to minimize 'reactivity' or observer effect, i.e. unnatural behaviour by the subjects of the research due to the presence of an outsider. Extreme examples of covert research have been reported by Hockey (1991), a former soldier who observed a group of young squaddies while he was a member of their troop, and Fielding (1981) who researched the National Front while masquerading as a member. Whether or not this could be achieved in education is debatable. It would be difficult for a researcher to pretend to be a school pupil. But a researcher could easily study a school or college staff while participating as a member of that staff, i.e. participant observation. Similarly (and this has happened in my own experience), a headteacher may even encourage a researcher to go into a classroom and play a different role, e.g. support teacher or visitor, in order to diminish the observer effect (reactivity).

One answer has been to involve 'collaborators' in the research. Farrell *et al.* (1988), for example, used a group of seven students to help them explore the lives of students in a high school, and how school fitted into their lives. These 'collaborators' interviewed fellow students and even helped to analyse the data.

There is a range of views on covert versus overt access, and positions in between (see Bulmer, 1982, for a good discussion). Some take a firm line, such as Maykut and Morehouse (1994, p. 70) who adopt the view that 'deceptive and covert practices are not in keeping with ethical practice'. Others adopt the line that deception is a price worth paying for minimizing the disturbance of a natural setting and thereby increasing 'validity' (see Scott and Usher, 1999, pp. 129–30 for a fuller discussion).

This is clearly an area where ethical and methodological issues overlap. The use of 'covert participant observation', or even some aspects of more overt participant observation, raises all sorts of ethical problems. My personal view is that the ethical guidelines put forward elsewhere in this book should prevail, and that openness and honesty are more important than gaining 'insider information' by deceptive means in order to increase so-called 'validity'.

IN SUMMARY: METAPHORS FOR THE RESEARCHER

A researcher has a wide range of roles and responsibilities in conducting educational research. The main responsibilities, perhaps, are to conduct the research ethically and reflectively. This involves researchers in pondering upon their role in conducting research. Various metaphors for the researcher can be, and have been, put forward: the researcher as participant; observer from a distance; market researcher; 'rambler' through an unknown terrain; detective; experimentalist; gardener; undercover policeman; and investigative journalist. In carrying out an enquiry, a researcher may play a role which relates to one or more of these metaphors.

Part 2: Methods and their Limits

Interviewing

INTRODUCTORY NOTES

Why Interview?

Interviewing people of any age can be one of the most enjoyable and interesting activities in a research study. Interviews can reach the parts which other methods cannot reach. Observation, for example, can allow us to study people's behaviour in 'strange' situations, such as classrooms or lecture theatres. Studying documents, such as a school or college prospectus, can allow a researcher to see the way an organization portrays itself in print. But interviewing allows a researcher to investigate and prompt things that we cannot observe. We can probe an interviewee's thoughts, values, prejudices, perceptions, views, feelings and perspectives. We can also elicit their version or their account of situations which they may have lived or taught through: his – or her – story.

Given that interviews are designed to elicit views and perspectives (the unobservable) it follows that their aim is not to establish some sort of inherent 'truth' in an educational situation. As postmodernist literature has discussed at considerable length, there are only 'multiple truths' in social situations, i.e. no single or absolute truth (see Usher and Edwards, 1994 and Hargreaves, 1994 for two useful accounts of 'postmodernism' in education).

Types and Styles of Interviewing

There are several different approaches to interviewing, therefore different ways of designing and structuring them and, in turn, different techniques for conducting them. These are discussed fully in this chapter.

Some authors have described interviews as 'a conversation with a purpose' (Webb and Webb, 1932). This approach involves a relatively informal, interactive style which may often involve a two-way exchange of views (e.g. Lather, 1986). There may be some sort of 'trading' going on, by which the interviewer puts as much in as he or she gets out of the interview.

At the opposite extreme, some researchers feel that an interviewer should act as a kind of sponge, soaking up the interviewee's comments and responses, i.e. the interviewer is a kind of data-collection device. An extreme example of this kind of interview is the experience which pedestrians in the high street are sometimes subjected to – the interviewer simply collects and records the responses of the passer-by without comment or feedback and often without any knowledge of the subject being studied.

In educational research the latter extreme is unlikely to occur. Any researcher will need to establish some kind of rapport with the interviewee (discussed later) and will necessarily have background knowledge and prior conceptions which are 'brought' to the research. However, my own view is that this does not imply a balanced, two-way exchange of views between interviewer and interviewee. The purpose of a research interview is to probe a respondent's views, perspectives or life-history, i.e. the exchange should be far more in one direction than another. It is rather more than a conversation with a purpose. The research interview's func-tion is to give a person, or group of people, a 'voice'. It should provide them with a 'platform', a chance to make their viewpoints heard and eventually read. It offers people, whether they be employ-ers, teachers, young pupils or students, an opportunity to make their perspectives known, i.e. to go public. In this sense an interview empowers people – the interviewer should not play the leading role.

This is my own view. Others' views will inevitably vary on the role of the interviewer and the 'best' style of interviewing. The style and approach to interviewing will also depend on the *purpose* of the research – as noted earlier, there is always an element of 'horses for courses' in educational research. In summary, there are various metaphors for the interviewer: a sponge; a sounding board; a prober; a listener; a counsellor; a recorder ('tabula rasa'); a challenger; a prompter; a sharer. They all need to be kept in mind and a flexible researcher may need to adopt different roles for different purposes, for different situations and with different interviewees. Interviewers will need to reveal something about themselves (and their motives and purposes) but should surely not treat the interview as *their* platform rather than the interviewee's.

Deciding on the Key Informants
The term 'key informant' has been used by anthropologists, and more particularly ethnographers, to describe the person who may be the key figure in a piece of qualitative research. In a true ethnographic study it may be an individual who

> is more sophisticated than his fellow informants, befriends the investigator, provides him with insights as well as detailed information, and acts generally as his mentor and guide for the duration of the study. (Richardson *et al.*, 1965, p. 114)

Similar expectations of a key informant are stated by Woods (1986, p. 85): 'key informants are people, with whom, over the course of the research, one comes to form an especially close relationship'. Such expectations of a key informant are perhaps easier to realize in a study which concentrates on one institution, or a small number, and also seeks to identify a particular group or sub-culture, as in some of the educational research described by Woods. However, the notion of 'key informant' is always an important one. There may be several key informants – some in different organizations, some at different levels within an organization. The aim for the researcher is to establish who are the key informants. For what purpose and for what perspective are they being interviewed? For example, it can be revealing to interview not only the personnel manager in a company but also one of the workers on the 'shop floor'. In a school, pupils' perspectives will often be as valuable as teachers', but what about non-teaching staff? Key informants at all 'levels' can be valuable in establishing different perspectives (see Schon, 1971) and also in creating some kind of 'in-house triangulation'.

Key informants may be subject to bias but this needs to be recognized:

> of course there may be forms of bias within our key informants. The usual safeguards apply to them, but it also helps to have various kinds of informants. The more they constitute a cross-section of the population in question, the easier we might feel about the danger of bias. (Woods, 1986, p. 86)

Data and results will still be influenced by the researcher's own perceptions and interpretations, however. This problem is considered later in discussing the quality of data and the recording of interviews.

If only one person is to be interviewed in an organization, e.g. a school, college or company, then it is vitally important to attempt to identify the key informant, e.g. the headteacher, the principal or the personnel manager. Le Compte (1984) describes key informants as: 'individuals who possess special knowledge, status or communication skills and who are willing to share that knowledge with the researcher'.

DEGREE OF STRUCTURE

A Matter of Degree
One of the issues that has featured most prominently in discussions of interviewing concerns the degree of structure in an interview. A distinction is often made between three degrees of structure (see, for example, Parsons, 1984):

1. In a structured situation the interview may be little more than a 'face-to-face questionnaire' (Parsons, 1984, p. 80). No deviation is made from either the wording or the order of a set list of questions. If properly administered such structure can be of value when a large number of interviewers are involved, e.g. in market research, and can provide a high 'degree of data quality and consistency' (*Ibid.*, p. 80).
2. At the other extreme, an unstructured interview, or non-standardized interview (Richardson *et al.*, 1965, p. 35), will vary from one interview and one interviewer to the next. There is no set list of questions or rigid order. As Parsons puts it, this approach resembles the 'probing or directed techniques adopted by the psychoanalyst' (1984, p. 81). Parsons warns against a totally unstructured approach in the data collection stage of research, although it may be valuable in the initial stages: 'The techniques may be valuable in early stages of the exploratory work but require a high level of interviewer expertise and in-depth understanding of the objectives of the survey.'
3. A compromise can be reached between the two positions which will overcome the problems inherent in the latter approach but avoid the inflexibility of the former. The compromise, although it can take various forms, can be referred to as the semi-structured interview. This general approach, although it depends greatly on the tactics and interaction discussed in the next section, is often the most valuable. The approach will involve some kind of interview guide or checklist. The interviewer has 'considerable flexibility over the range and order of questions within a loosely defined framework' (*Ibid.*, p. 80). The guidelines may involve a checklist of

issues to be covered, or even a checklist of questions. Degrees of structure will vary enormously within the framework, depending on the expertise of the interviewers and their interaction with the interviewees. For example, in ethnographic interviewing (discussed shortly) the structure and path of the interview will be dictated as much by the respondent as by the questioner. Roles may be revised or reversed if a true rapport is established. This vital feature of interviewing, which is perhaps more important than either a rigid prior structure or a general framework, is discussed in the next section.

Table 5.1 below gives a summary of the three degrees of structure in interviewing.

Table 5.1: Styles of interviewing

Unstructured	Semi-structured	Structured
Some 'control' on both sides	More control by interviewer	Most control by interviewer
Very flexible	Flexible	Less flexible
Guided by the interviewee	Not completely pre-determined	Guided by researcher's pre-determined agenda
Direction unpredictable		More predictable
May be difficult to analyse		May provide easier framework for analysis

Interview Guides and Interview Schedules
In some extreme cases of interview-based research, it may be possible, and productive, to start with one single, key question to act as a trigger for the rest of the interview. Perry (1970) reports a piece of research investigating college students' experiences of their own development in their 'college years'. To start the interview he first welcomed the student, expressed his interest in hearing about their college experiences and then simply asked: 'Why don't you start with whatever stands out for you about the year?' This acted as a launch-pad for the rest of the interview, which then relied on the skill of the interviewer to elicit, elaborate on and probe the students' responses.

Such an approach depends heavily on the social and communication skills of the interviewer. A more common approach is to

Table 5.2: Forming interview guides and interview schedules

Stage 1	Brainstorming: jumbled, unjudged list of ideas, questions, areas of interest
Stage 2	Classifying and categorizing: areas, topics, questions are grouped into classes or categories ('categories of inquiry')
Stage 3	Interview guide: selection and judgement on which areas/questions will actually be explored
Stage 4	Interview schedule: phrasing of all questions into meaningful language, e.g. for school pupils; removing ambiguity; careful sequencing of questions; identifying and ordering closed and open questions

Source: Discussed fully in Maykut and Morehouse (1994, pp. 83–94)

formulate a set of key questions which the researcher wishes to follow in an interview. The first step is to create an *interview guide* (Patton, 1990). This is a classified list of the topics – the issues or broad research questions which the researcher intends to explore. The best way to start this is to brainstorm using a large piece of paper, or better still, as a research team using a flipchart or a whiteboard (if there is no research team, a student could work with a supervisor, a colleague or a friend).

Brainstorming will yield a jumbled collection of areas of interest, questions, interesting topics, words, phrases and so on (see Table 5.2).

The next stage is to start to classify and categorize these ideas or questions. Maykut and Morehouse (1994, p. 84) call these 'categories of inquiry'. These are put into groups or clusters and then a selection is made before transferring the categories of inquiry onto a new sheet of paper. This forms the interview guide.

For some researchers, this may be enough to take out into the field. But for many the next step is to convert it into an *interview schedule*. This involves first turning all the ideas or areas of inquiry into meaningful questions for the target interviewees. It involves careful use of language, e.g. avoidance of jargon and careful phrasing. The questions need to make sense and be unambiguous.

Some questions will be closed, i.e. capable of having only one answer, e.g. age, gender, number of years' teaching experience. This basic information is often necessary at the start of an interview and can be a good way of getting started or warming up. But in an interview the primary purpose, as discussed earlier, is to probe people's views, perspectives, experiences and so on. Hence many of the questions in an interview will be open questions.

The knack of developing a good interview schedule is to sequence it with the easy, closed questions early on and the more difficult open questions requiring a good deal of thought and introspection towards the end. Start simple and build up to a crescendo!

TACTICS, APPROACH AND PRACTICALITIES

Preliminaries

Any interviewer will need to be aware of certain necessary preliminaries before interviewing, whatever the style and structure of the interview. Some of these are practicalities, some are ethical requirements.

- First, if planning to tape-record an interview, permission should always be sought. It is not acceptable to tape-record interviews (or observations) without the subjects' prior knowledge and permission. If the subject feels uncomfortable or simply does not wish to have his/her voice taped, that wish must be upheld.
- Secondly, every assurance should be made (and later kept, especially when writing up) to preserve the subject's anonymity and the confidentiality of their responses.
- Thirdly, the interviewees should be given the essential information about the research study itself. Why are you doing it? Who (if anybody) is funding it? Why were *they* chosen to be interviewed and not somebody else? How long will it take? Who are you and why are you interested in this field? What will happen to the notes/recording, and will they be able to see them for verification?

These are all points which must be covered as a necessary preliminary to an interview. The respondents have a right to receive these assurances and to have their questions answered, even if it adds a few minutes to the time required.

Box 5.1 gives a summary of the main stages in preparing for and carrying out interviews.

Rapport

One of the first tasks of an interviewer is to establish a rapport with the interviewee. Smith (1972) suggests that 'rapport' should be the 'result of a positive, pleasant, yet business-like approach' (p. 20). She distinguishes task involvement in an interview – i.e. involvement with the questions and answers related to the business at hand – from social involvement, i.e. involvement with the interviewee at a personal level. Smith argues that the former (task involvement) should be as high as possible, and the latter as low as possible. This

Box 5.1: Stages in preparing and carrying out interviews

---

1. Preparing the interview schedule
- Translating research objectives/questions into interview questions
- Deciding the degree of structure (see Table 5.1)
- Ordering the questions, e.g. closed to open-ended
- Deciding how the responses will be collected (tape versus note taking: see Box 5.3)

2. Piloting
- Practising/trying out on a small sample
- Eliminating ambiguous, confusing or insensitive questions

3. Selecting the subjects/sample
- Choosing a representative, sensible sample
- Negotiating access and suitable venue, with individuals and institutions

4. The interview itself
- Physical positioning and preparation, i.e. side-by-side or face-to-face? Tape recording or note taking?
- Briefing and explanation, e.g. purpose of the interview and the research generally; how the data will be used; anonymity
- Questioning
- Rounding up, thanks, future contact, feedback

---

is sound advice, although it should not be interpreted too rigidly. The need to establish rapport is vital, and the ease with which it can be established will vary according to the ease of interaction of the parties, the venue of the interview and the personal interests and backgrounds of both the interviewer and the interviewee. The skilled interviewer, therefore, should be able to assess the balance needed between task involvement and social involvement in relation to those variables.

Questioning, Probing and Prompting

At least four issues are important here: the use of leading questions, open and closed questioning, ambiguity, and the distinction between probing and prompting. These issues overlap so they will be considered together.

An interview is likely to contain a mixture of open and closed questions. Open questions will be included in order to seek opinions, to invite the interviewee to express views and attitudes or to encourage prediction or sheer speculation, e.g. on future needs, new developments etc. This extreme of open-ended questioning contrasts with the tightly closed question asking simply for a specific piece of information, e.g. the number of employees in a firm, number of students enrolled, numbers of staff. If an open-ended question is asked in a leading way, e.g. 'Do you feel that higher education fails to make sufficient contact with industry?', it is likely to bias interview results. It could also be argued that a seemingly open question phrased in a leading manner is in essence a 'closed' question anyway. A genuinely open question will invite opinions or views without either leading or prompting (see Box 5.2).

Parsons (1984) makes the distinction between probing and prompting as follows:

> Prompting the respondent is a dangerous technique for structured interviews, and should be rigorously avoided. Probing, by contrast, is not only permissible but it is doubtful if anything but the simplest interviews could be completed without it. At first sight the distinction between the two may seem marginal, even pedantic. In essence, prompting indirectly leads the respondents: 'Do you mean that …?', which may cause some bias in the reply; whilst probing is neutral: 'Could you tell me more about …?'. (p. 89)

The value of probing was stressed in an earlier handbook for interviewers, which defined a probe as 'any stimulus which is not a prompt, applied in order to obtain a response from an informant or a more extensive or explicit expression of it' (Atkinson, 1968).

Probes can be of different kinds. The first could be called a 'tell me more' probe. This could be seeking further elaboration or expansion of a particular viewpoint or an anecdote, or it could be asking for more detail or more precise information, e.g. 'Exactly how many pupils were involved?'

A second type of probe can be called a 'getting clearer' probe. You may not follow the language used, e.g. jargon, slang; you may need clarification about the situation or the context; you may simply not understand.

Patton (1990) labels three types of probes, similar to my categories. He calls them detail-oriented probes, elaboration probes and clarification probes. A useful discussion of these probes is given by Maykut and Morehouse (1994, pp. 95–6).

In any event the interviewer needs to use a probe carefully and sensitively, i.e. politely.

Probing, as opposed to prompting, can clearly be valuable in open-ended questioning. However, some authors have warned against its use for two reasons. First, it can, if taken too far, result in 'over-probing'. The interviewee may be goaded into certain responses, again resulting in bias due to the interviewer (Moser, 1958). Many interviewers feel that probing should therefore be non-directive, as opposed to leading or directive (see Brenner *et al.*, 1985, p. 25). Other authors have warned against the use of open-ended questions in interviewing, not only because of the danger of overprobing but also because of the difficulty of analysing the data (Smith, 1972, p. 23). However, in my view, the sheer quality and vividness of the data collected in open-ended questioning, e.g. in capturing 'the texture of reality' (Stenhouse, 1979) outweighs these difficulties.

A final problem in questioning is the danger of ambiguity which again could affect the quality of the data. This is perhaps less of a problem in interviewing – certainly when rapport has been established – than in, say, a postal survey. Interviewees should be able to clear up any ambiguity by asking for clarification or by probing the interviewer themselves, e.g. 'Could you explain your meaning of the term "information technology"?' or 'What do you mean by ...?' This is certainly one of the strengths of a reflexive style of interviewing, discussed shortly. The possibility of removing ambiguity and lack of clarity is also the main advantage of a personal interview (which is essentially interactive) over a postal questionnaire which is essentially non-interactive.

A useful summary of handy hints to remember when questioning is given by Anderson, G. (1990, p. 236) and discussed further by him. These hints or tips apply equally to interviewing and to questionnaires (see Chapter 7).

Ethnographic Interviewing
Some of the points discussed above in considering tactics and approaches are covered by Hammersley and Atkinson (1983, p. 112) under their heading of 'ethnographic interviewing'. They suggest that the style, structure and even the questions asked should be a product of interaction between the researcher and informant, i.e. 'interviewing should be reflexive rather than standardised'. As a result, the approach may vary from directive to non-directive at appropriate times. In testing a developing hypothesis, for example, directive questioning and probing (discussed earlier) may be needed. (A full discussion of ethnographic interviewing and its relation to participant observation is given in Hammersley and Atkinson, 1983, pp. 112–26.)

Group Interviewing
It should not be taken for granted that interviewing is best done in one-to-one, interviewer-to-interviewee situations. Group interviews

in which an interviewer talks with, say, three or four people together can often have advantages. The interviewees may feel safer, more secure and at ease if they are with their peers (this may be especially true of infants, or even teenagers or teachers). They are also more likely to relax, 'warm-up' and jog each other's memories and thoughts.

On the other hand, group interviewing has potential disadvantages: the maverick voice or the long monologue; dominant individuals who may monopolize the interview or invisibly 'threaten' the others by their presence; the reduction in time devoted to each individual; the person who is afraid to speak in a group. These disadvantages need skilful management, even control, if they are to be avoided. Seating also needs to be carefully arranged to allow proper eye contact and, of course, the strategic location of a microphone, if the session is to be taped. (Incidentally, a group interview requires a higher quality recording system than a one-to-one interview.)

One other strategy which I have found valuable and enjoyable is for two researchers to interview jointly a group of young people. This may seem labour-intensive but it has many benefits: an extra perspective on the interviewer 'side', leading, perhaps, to fuller and richer questioning; the chance for interviewees to interact with two people, e.g. a male and a female interviewer, thus doubling the chance of empathy; if one interviewer becomes tired, inattentive or loses concentration for a short time the other can 'take over'; two people listening and recording can share their perspectives afterwards; one person may 'pick things up', e.g. body language, group interactions, tone of voice, which the other has missed (with a structured, scheduled interview an interviewing pair are less likely to miss items); one person can listen, record or even take a breather while the other questions and manages the group, and vice versa. In short, two interviewers working together can have several advantages and may help to improve the quality of the data.

THE QUALITY OF DATA

Factors Affecting Quality

A large number of factors, many of which are related to the execution of an interview mentioned above, will affect the quality of the data collected (the question of whether the term 'data' or 'evidence' should be used is considered shortly).

First, as mentioned earlier, the interaction between interviewer and interviewee is crucial. If 'social involvement' is too high then bias may result (Smith, 1972, p. 20). However, sufficient rapport should be established between the parties, enhanced by some degree of social interaction, in order to allow any ambiguity or lack of clarity to be sorted.

Ambiguity in questions, as several authors note (e.g. Richardson *et al.*, 1965, p. 246), is a major source of error, as is lack of agreement over the meanings of the terms being used (see Box 5.2). Another factor affecting quality is the use of leading questions or excessive prompting during interviewing. This may lead to bias, although some writers on ethnography have suggested that leading questions are inevitable in developing 'grounded theory' (Hammersley and Atkinson, 1983; Glaser and Strauss, 1967).

Box 5.2: Five types of questions to avoid

---

1. **Double-barrelled questions**
   Avoid double-barrelled questions, e.g. 'Have you ever experienced severe stress and what did you do to cope with it?'
   Ask one question at a time. Do not combine questions and expect an answer.

2. **Two-in-one questions**
   Do not combine opposite positions in one question, e.g. 'What are the advantages and disadvantages of working in an independent school?'
   Separate out the parts.

3. **Restrictive questions**
   Avoid questions which inherently eliminate some options, e.g. 'Do you think that female school headteachers are as good as male school heads?' (This question eliminates the possibility that women might be better.)
   Avoid 'double-question' questions, e.g. 'Do you ever feel irritated and depressed by your students?' The respondent might be irritated but not depressed, or vice versa, or both, or neither.

4. **Leading questions**
   Do not precede questions with a position statement. In this type of question, the interviewer states a view or summarizes a position and then asks for a response. This could lead the respondent in a given direction.

5. **Loaded questions**
   Avoid questions which are emotionally charged and use loaded words, e.g. 'Would you favour or oppose murder by agreeing with a woman's free choice concerning abortion?'

Source: adapted from Anderson, G. (1990)

Other sources of error are discussed at length by Smith (1972, pp. 19–26). She suggests two additional sources of error in interviewing: an overlong schedule leading to inattention and fatigue; and 'cheating' on the part of the interviewer or interviewee, e.g. distortion of the truth.

A major source of error, which will be discussed shortly, can occur in making records of interviews. This will occur whether notes are taken during interview or transcription is made later from a tape recording, or even if both methods are used.

The important point to note from this section is that any interviewer should be aware of errors that are likely to occur and should take as many steps as possible to increase the quality of the data. This can be achieved as much by a reflective and critical approach to interviewing (with the above factors in mind) as by careful prior formulation of the interview schedule or by piloting and consequent revision of questions.

Data or Evidence?

The information collected through interview is often termed data. However, an important distinction can be made between interviewing for 'data' and interviewing for 'evidence'. Roizen and Jepson (1985) discuss this distinction by quoting Stenhouse (1978):

> The alternative style of interviewing which is my concern here has as its objective to elicit, not data, but evidence. When we interview for data, we attempt to gather information whose reliability and status is defined by the process of data gathering. When we interview for evidence our aim is to gather information whose reliability and status is left problematic and has to be established by critical comparison and scrutiny. Meaning is ascribed to information by critical interpretation: its reliability or status is assessed by critical verification. The process of critical verification and interpretation is one familiar to the historian.
>
> The objective of the interviewer who is gathering evidence must be to evoke extensive and naturally expressed information because rich texture and contextualisation is necessary if an adequate critique is to be mounted. Moreover, vivid natural discourse may be needed to support communication with the reader to whom the researcher appeals for verification of his own judgements by presenting evidence. The reportage of research in this tradition is not a presentation of results, but of interpretation accessible to reflection or discussion.

Stenhouse's concern for accessibility of evidence and the issue of verification is considered again later. His distinction between data and evidence is surely a valuable one.

INTERVIEW RECORDS

The recording of interviews may involve note taking, more detailed record-keeping, tape recording or, in some cases, photographic or video records (on the latter, see Walker and Adelman, 1972). The more involved process of developing a 'case record' of an organization involving notes, documents, annual reports and transcripts of interviews will be considered under the discussion of Case Study (see Chapter 6). The main issues here are the accuracy of recording methods and the influence of perceptions and interpretation in transcribing interviews. The latter issue is connected with the earlier discussion of 'data' and 'evidence'. Roizen and Jepson (1985) argue, in agreement with Stenhouse (1978), that the transcription of interviews from tape is problematic and that the term 'evidence', not data, should be used to signify interview records:

> Each transcription is a single opinion or perception which gains weight from its consistency with other pieces of evidence or gains utility in allowing the analyst to further the empirical differentiation of key concepts. The problem is reducibility and choice. With respect to reducibility it is a matter of retaining the life and texture of the original source. The transcripts often are ambiguous on a problem area, sometimes inconsistent, sometimes inarticulate. Almost always an argument is multi-dimensional. Over-refinement of the evidence presents an artificial clarity of view. (Roizen and Jepson, 1985, p. 11)

One solution may be to transcribe an interview in its entirety, word for word. This may avoid 'over-refinement' and 'artificial clarity' but it will provide a massive volume of data (or evidence) which is too verbose either to analyse or report. Woods (1986) suggests two stages in transcription which may help to overcome the above problems. First, the whole tape can be listened to while notes on, even an index of, its contents can be made. Initial selection can then be made by the interviewer so that, in the second stage, either the whole or special parts of the interview can be transcribed. This initial selection, made through the eyes (or ears), and from the perspective of the researcher, is the first step in the analysis and interpretation of data. Selective attention is thus being paid to data, but this is a feature of any systematic research, not least scientific research where observation is blatantly theory-laden (Popper, 1963).

Field notes made during interviews will be a valuable aid in transcribing from tape – these notes should also provide information

on the time and place, the setting and impressions of the interviewee's position, disposition, attitude, and so on (see Woods, 1986,
pp. 81–2, for a full discussion).

I have suggested here that notes and tape recording can be used
together in interviewing to improve accuracy and quality of data/
evidence, and to enrich the 'texture of reality' (Stenhouse, 1978) in
presenting this type of research. However, the use of mechanical aids,
be they audio or video, may be seen as obtrusive in some situations.
Pupils, employers or teachers, for example, may not wish their views
to be recorded on tape, particularly if they are forthright (or even
unprintable) or if they are at odds with other informants. The use of
an aid such as a tape recorder should, therefore, always be negotiated
with a special eye on the issue of data privacy or anonymity.

On the other hand (as I have found in my own experience) the use
of a tape recorder (particularly if it is of high-quality) is often seen as a
compliment by the person being interviewed. This accords with
Stenhouse's hope (1984, p. 26) that 'the occasion is slightly flattering
to the person being interviewed'. The flattery is increased by the use
of a purpose-built recorder and copious note taking. In a sense, the
interviewer is providing a platform for the respondent to express
himself or herself. In Stenhouse's words,

> Part of my job is to give people the feeling not merely that they
> have my ear, my mind, and my thoughts concentrated on them
> but that they want to give an account of themselves because they
> see the interview as in some way an opportunity: an opportunity
> of telling someone how they see the world. (p. 222)

Finally, careful recording and processing of interview records can
enhance and encourage respondent validation, i.e. returning a well-
prepared interview record (or in some cases observation record) to
the informant for appraisal and checking. The value of respondent
validation is stressed by Woods (1986, p. 86):

> There are two levels at which this might prove useful. Firstly, in
> checking the accuracy of the data. Have you got the report of
> that event straight? Are certain impressions fairly represented?
> Have all relevant points been taken into account? Secondly, on
> any interpretation or explanation, the informant may have some
> useful comments to make.

Box 5.3 gives a summary of the relative merits of tape recording
versus note taking in interviewing. My personal view is that it is
generally best to record interviews on tape (given the interviewee's

Box 5.3: Tape recording versus note taking

Tape recording	
Advantages	Disadvantages
• Preserves actual natural language, i.e. a verbatim account • Can be flattering for interviewee • Is an 'objective' record • Interviewer's contribution is also recorded and can be reflected upon • Allows interviewer to concentrate, to maintain eye contact and to observe body language	• Can generate enormous amounts of data • Time-consuming to transcribe • Context not recorded • Presence of machine can be off-putting, e.g. creates anxiety • Core issues may be masked by irrelevancies
Note taking	
Advantages	Disadvantages
• Central issues/facts recorded • Economical • Off-record statements not recorded	• Recorder bias • Can be distracting for the interviewee • Encoding may interfere with interview • Status of data may be questioned (i.e. difficult to verify)

Source: Based in part on Nunan, 1992, p. 153

permission) if only so that researchers can analyse and reflect initially upon their own interviewing style and technique.

THE GENERATION OF THEORY

The generation of theory is a key issue not only for interviewing but for qualitative research itself and, more generally, for any research process. In this section the specific role of interviewing in relation to the somewhat problematic notion of 'theory' is considered briefly, although the discussion of theory has application to other research methods.

Roizen and Jepson (1986, p. 7) suggest that 'qualitative research is often concerned with the development or revision of concepts'. This is particularly true of interviewing, especially in an unstructured, exploratory form. The purpose of an interview is often to clarify meanings, to examine concepts or to discover areas of ambiguity. This can be achieved in an interview which is truly interactive and reflexive (Hammersley and Atkinson, 1983). With such an approach, 'the respondent typically has some measure of control over the research process' (Roizen and Jepson, p. 7). In the case of Roizen and Jepson's (1986) research into employer expectations of higher education, they were searching not only for clarification of meanings and concepts but also for some sort of typology of instances and arguments:

> What is gathered and analysed is evidence which shows the range and types of instances of arguments, analysis and conceptual variation in employers' perceptions, opinions and behaviour in respect of higher education.

For example, a study of employers' needs in new technology might include the concepts of 'skill shortages', 'prior requirement', 'new technology', 'poaching' (of personnel) or even 'qualification' (Wellington, 1989). The actual use, or in some cases lack of use, of such concepts is a useful starting point in developing 'theory' and in going on to use more quantitative or large-volume research methods. This prior development of conceptual clarification and theoretical perspectives was seen as their main aim by Roizen and Jepson (1985, p. 8):

> The main focus of this study is not theoretical. We are not in the first instance aiming to test hypotheses against the evidence. Rather we are trying to develop the meaning and empirical content of concepts useful to a number of theoretical perspectives.

Typology and conceptual clarification, however, are in a sense only a starting point towards the development of theory from research. In a way they are reminiscent of John Locke's metaphor of the philosopher as an 'underlabourer' clearing away the undergrowth a little or hacking through the conceptual jungle before the real empirical work could be done (see Locke, 1690 and Gilroy, 1980, for a critique). Bulmer (1979, p. 6) makes a similar point:

> Concepts in themselves are not theories. They are categories for the organization of ideas and observations. In order to form an explanatory theory, concepts must be interrelated. But concepts do act as a means of storing observations of phenomena which may at a future time be used in theory ... Concepts then mediate between theory and data. They form an essential bridge, but one which is difficult to construct and maintain.

The discussion so far leaves the question of theory generation unanswered; it has merely pointed to the important role of interviewing in clarifying concepts and, at most, suggesting theoretical perspectives. One problem in taking this discussion further is that the notion of theory is itself problematic and is the topic of a huge body of literature and research, not least in the philosophy of science (for an overview see Popper, 1963; Kuhn, 1970; Chalmers, 1982; to quote a tiny sample). That debate cannot be explored here, but at least three types of theory can be usefully distinguished for this context:

1. Descriptive theory – its main purpose being to explain what is happening;
2. Explanatory theory – explaining why it is happening and perhaps enabling predictions (predictive theory); and
3. 'Grounded' theory – a notion first developed by Glaser and Strauss (1967).

Commentators on qualitative research (e.g. Yin, 1984) have argued that explanatory theory can best be developed by the use of case studies which are considered shortly. Yin discusses the 'familiar series' of research questions, which he labels who, what, where, how and why (*Ibid.*, p. 17). He suggests that case study is most effective in searching for causes, i.e. in answering 'why' questions, while survey methods perhaps serve a more descriptive purpose, i.e. in considering 'what' questions. Both methods are considered later in this book.

The notion of 'grounded theory' is an even more difficult one to consider adequately, particularly as it now seems to be the foundation for a whole research tradition. Perhaps its essential tenet is that theory should be generated 'in the field' and continually tested further by data collection which is, in turn, guided by theoretical sampling. In other words, theory is both determined by and a determinant of data collection.

To give a concrete example that might illustrate types of theory, a study of employers' recruitment trends in new technology might reveal an increasing trend towards graduate recruitment. A study of the causes of this trend, perhaps by interview and also by case study, might suggest the following explanatory theories which are grounded firmly in the increasing evidence gathered:

1. that the trend is caused by developments in the technology itself;
2. that the increasing polarization of skills is one of the causes of the trend; and

3. that the desire of firms to improve the general quality of their labour force has led to increased graduate recruitment.

Such theories, or rather explanations, would be grounded and would also be susceptible to checking and reshaping as research progressed (Wellington, 1989). Further sampling would be theoretical in the sense that it 'exposed' those theories to the test (to use Popper's metaphor).

The discussion of theory cannot be pursued further here. One of the most interesting discussions was provided by Woods (1986, chapters 6 and 7).

Case studies

This chapter will cover a range of different aspects of case study research. Many of the issues already raised, e.g. problems of access, gaining entry, sampling and the role of theory also apply to this section but will not be rehearsed again. The section begins with a discussion of the notion of case study and goes on to consider different aspects of the study of cases. Bogdan and Biklen (1982) provide a useful account of how research work may lead into case study:

> The general design of a case study is best represented by a funnel. The start of the study is the wide end: the researchers scout for possible places and people that might be the subject or the source of data, find the location they think they want to study, and then cast a net widely trying to judge the feasibility of the site or data source for their purposes.

Eventually, a focus develops at the narrow end of the 'funnel' and the case study begins.

THE MEANING OF 'CASE STUDY'

A large amount has been written on the use of case study within the huge body of literature on qualitative research. The notion of 'case study' has been widely discussed. Bogdan and Biklen (1982, p. 58) offer a suitable operative definition: 'A case study is a detailed examination of one setting, or one single subject, or one single depository of documents, or one particular event.' Note the stress on the unit. The unit may be a school (or even a setting within it) in educational research. It could even be one person, e.g. a student in a school or college. In a study of employers' needs, each 'employing organization' could make up a single case. This is, at once, the strength and, some may argue, the weakness of the case study, i.e. the importance of the context of the unit and the consequent problematic nature of generalization. As Stenhouse (1985, p. 266) points out:

> In case study the relationship between a case, or a collection of cases that may superficially resemble a sample, and any population in which similar meanings or relationships may apply, is essentially a matter of judgement.

He goes on to argue that this is the strength of case study:

> Case study reaches after the restoration of prudence, and also of perceptiveness, the capacity to interpret situations rapidly and at depth and to revise interpretations in the light of experience.

The problem of generalizability will of course depend on the nature of the case study itself and the choice of units (this is discussed in a later section).

Box 6.1 gives a summary of what might count as a case study.

Box 6.1: What might count as a 'case study'?

1. An account of one individual or one classroom, e.g. Armstrong, M. (1980): a diary of one primary classroom.
2. An account of two or more individuals, e.g. Edwards, J. (1994): 'The scars of dyslexia' (8 boys); Turkle, S. (1984): 'The second self' (a large number of computer users/hackers).
3. A study of one organization, e.g. Ball, S. (1981): Beachside Comprehensive; Lacey, C. (1970): Hightown Grammar; Walford, G and Miller, H. (1991): City Technology College.
4. A study of two or more organizations, e.g. schools, employers, e.g. Wright, C. (1992), on four primary schools; Wellington, J. (1989), on five employers.
5. An account of one or more groups, e.g. a family or a community, e.g. Whyte, W.F. (1981): *Street Corner Society.*
6. A study of specific events or relationships, e.g. Woods, P. (1993), on 'critical events'; Tripp, D. (1993), on 'critical incidents'.

(See Appendix 1 for further details on Armstrong, Edwards, Ball and Lacey.)

TYPES OF CASE STUDY

Both Stenhouse (1985) and Bogdan and Biklen (1982) provide useful classifications of case study. The latter distinguish three major categories: historical–organizational case studies; observational case studies; and the life history form of case study. The first involves studies of a unit, e.g. an organization, over a period, thereby tracing its development. This may involve interviews with people who have been involved with the organization over a lengthy period and also a study of written records. Bogdan and Biklen (p. 59) point out that satisfactory studies of this kind are rare, often because sources are insufficient.

The second category involves largely participant observation of an organization. Observational case studies will often include a historical aspect but this is 'supplementary to a concern with the contemporary scene'. Finally, a life history form of case study will involve extensive interviews with 'one person for the purpose of collecting a first person narrative' (Bogdan and Biklen, 1982, p. 61). A broader notion of the life history method is discussed in Woods (1985, p. 164) who cites the work of Faraday and Plummer (1979). Woods suggests that the life history method may undergo a revival in popularity but he also points out some of its weaknesses, e.g. in the development of theory.

Stenhouse (1985, p. 226) makes a similar distinction of two traditions in case study: historical and ethnographic, and suggests that 'there is a sense in which history is the work of insiders, ethnography of outsiders'. The study of, for example, a new organization will necessarily involve an outsider's perspective, although life history interviews (indeed interviews of any kind with key informants) could assist with providing the insider's view.

Finally, for this section, Stake (1994) makes a distinction between three types of case study which can sometimes be useful:

1. The *intrinsic case study*, undertaken in order to gain a better understanding of this particular case, not because the case is unique or typical but because it is of interest in itself:

   The purpose is not to come to understand some abstract phenomenon, such as literacy or teenage drug use or what a school principal does. The purpose is not theory building … Study is undertaken because of an intrinsic interest in, for example, this particular child, clinic, conference, or curriculum. (p. 237)

2. The *instrumental case study*, used to provide insight into a particular issue or to clarify a hypothesis. The actual case is secondary – its aim is to develop our understanding and knowledge of something else: 'The choice of case is made because it is expected to advance our understanding of that other interest.' (*Idem*)

   However, separating intrinsic case studies from instrumental case studies is often difficult: 'there is no line distinguishing intrinsic case study from instrumental; rather a zone of combined purpose separates them'. (*Idem*)

3. The *collective case study* – the study of a number of different cases. The cases may have similar or dissimilar characteristics but they are chosen in order that theories can be generated about a larger collection of cases. In this way they employ a very different mode of thinking from the single case study.

The extent to which observation in case study could provide a varying perspective is considered next.

OBSERVATION AND PARTICIPANT OBSERVATION

A case study of an organization may well involve observation, discussion, interviewing, visits to different sites and the study of written records and documentation. The nature of observation has been widely discussed, particularly by commentators of ethnography. The key phrase often associated with ethnography is 'participant observation' (see, for example, Spradley (1980) and numerous others listed below). This may be possible to achieve in some settings but, as mentioned in Stenhouse's comment earlier, some aspects of case study inevitably involve the perception of an 'outsider'. Participant observation is difficult to achieve. A useful framework for considering observation in different settings is drawn up in Hammersley and Atkinson (1983, p. 93) and has been adapted into the spectrum shown in Figure 6.1.

Different kinds of observation from this spectrum may be possible to achieve in different situations. This will depend on a number of variables. In a long-term study of an organization, for example, an observer may gradually become more and more of a participant. Participant observation requires time, acceptance, carefully negotiated access and tact, problems all discussed at length by commentators on ethnographic method from Glaser and Strauss (1967) to Woods (1986).

The role of 'complete participant' has often occurred where the

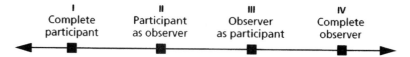

Figure 6.1: A spectrum of observation

researcher's activities are wholly concealed from the group being studied. This has happened in studies of a Glasgow gang (Patrick, 1973), the police force (Holdaway, 1985) and in studies of the army, alcoholics and a mental hospital mentioned in Hammersley and Atkinson (1983).

Shorter case studies, on the other hand, are likely to entail far more observation than participation. These could involve visits to organizations, a study of their documentation, interviews and discussions with staff (and/or students) and other sources of 'evidence' which are discussed below.

OTHER ASPECTS OF CASE STUDY

Observation, with whatever degree of participation, is clearly an important part of case study. But equally important is the role of interviewing (considered at length earlier), discussion with people at all possible levels, and the use of documentation of all kinds. Together these sources allow a 'picture' to be built up of the case being studied which allows a piece of research to capture 'the texture of reality' (Stenhouse, 1979) so important in providing a useful presentation when findings are disseminated. The type of record built up is often called a 'case record' and this notion is discussed shortly.

A case study can often involve a study of resources within an organization. This may involve looking at equipment (hardware or software), room design (e.g. open plan working) and management of human resources (e.g. team versus individual working). The general level and standard of resourcing will be an interesting feature of case study and can be gauged partly by direct observation, but also by collecting evidence from written material or by interviewing key informants.

Finally, a case study can involve an appraisal or simply a 'feel for' the style and the ethos of an organization. This is something that can be gauged as much by intuition as by structured observation or interviewing.

Impression and intuition, interviewing and observation, and the study of documentation all form part of the 'case record', a notion which is considered next.

Box 6.2 gives a summary of the various sources of data which might go towards this record.

Box 6.2: Data collection in case study: a summary of commonly used techniques

---

1. Observation
(a) *Participant observation*: the researcher is more than a passive observer and participates in the events being studied.
(b) *Systematic observation*: use of standardized observation instrument.
(c) *Simple observation*: passive, unobtrusive observation (e.g. of facial expression, language use, behaviour).
2. Interview
(a) *Structured interview*: set of predetermined questions in a set order.
(b) *Focused/semi-structured interview*: interview schedule specifying key areas but order of questions not fixed.
(c) *Open-ended interview*: no pre-specified schedule or order of questions; little direction from interviewer.
3. Use of documents and records
Includes a wide range of written or recorded materials, e.g. minutes of meetings, pupil records, diaries, school brochures, reports.
4. A wide range of other techniques including questionnaires; standardized tests (e.g. of intelligence, personality or attainment); scales (e.g. of attitude); repertory grids; life histories; role play, simulation and gaming.

Source: adapted from Robson, 1993, p. 159

MAKING CASE RECORDS

Roizen and Jepson (1985, p. 10) describe their conception of a case record in their own study of employers' expectations of higher education:

> For each organisation a 'case record' was developed. From such records the individual pieces of evidence were selected for presentation. The case record created by the interviewers included: transcripts or partial transcripts of interviews; annual reports; published descriptions of the firm; and newspaper articles covering the period of the research. In addition, each interview included contextual descriptive material on the employing organisation, on the mode of recruiting graduates, on the effects of the economic recession on the firm, etc. Although not all of this material is included in the analysis presented, it formed the analytic framework used to select and interpret the evidence.

Perhaps the key sentence is the last one; a vast amount of material is built up in a case record. Although only a part of it is likely to be presented in a final report, thesis or manageable publication of any kind, it does provide the framework for that publication.

A similar point is made by Rudduck (1985, p. 102) in her discussion of case records. She talks of three stages in case study research: the case data, the case record and the case study. In multi-site research, a fourth stage may be involved 'which seeks generalizations across case records' (*Ibid.*, p. 103, also discussed by Bogdan and Biklen, 1982, pp. 65–8).

Rudduck, in discussing Stenhouse's view of case study methodology, describes the 'case data' as the totality of the material collected, while the 'case record' is a 'lightly edited, ordered, indexed and public version of the case data'. Thus the case record may include edited notes, reports of observations, transcripts of interviews and, of course, documents, reports or any other published material, including perhaps photographic material.

The case study is, then (in Rudduck's words), 'the product of the field worker's reflective engagement with an individual case record' (p. 103). Case records are thus 'relatively untheorised and lightly edited' in comparison with a case study which is, in a sense, a stage of interpretation and reflection further on. The notion of a case record was developed by Stenhouse (1978) as a way of allowing verification in case study work:

> no qualitatively based theorising in education should be acceptable unless its argument stands or falls on the interpretation of accessible and well-cited sources, so that the interpretation offered can be critically examined.

The availability of case records which are publicly accessible and 'as raw as possible' (Rudduck, 1985, p. 104) will allow the interpretation of data or evidence to be verified. This assumes that the act of data gathering or observation is itself interpretation, or theory-free. This has, of course, been the subject of much debate. Nevertheless, the notion of case records leading to a more refined case study is one which can be usefully adopted.

The product of the researcher's immersion in, analysis of and reflection on the case record is the case study itself – the written report.

A case study should be enjoyable and interesting to read. Readers should be able to 'learn lessons from it' (Anderson, G., 1990). The ability to relate to a case and learn from it is perhaps more important than being able to generalize from it.

ADVANTAGES AND DISADVANTAGES OF CASE STUDY

Case study research has a large number of attractions and advantages, in addition to the fact that it can be enjoyable to do. Case studies can be illuminating and insightful; if well written, they can be attention-holding and exude a strong sense of reality; they are often accessible and engaging for readers; case studies derived from research can be of great value in teaching and learning; case studies can lead to subsequent quantitative research by pointing to issues which can or should be investigated over a wider range; they can also follow on from a broader survey or quantitative approach by exploring a phenomenon in greater depth – in a more exploratory, explanation-seeking fashion, and thereby enrich it.

Table 6.1 sums up some of the main alleged strengths, and the alleged weaknesses, of case study research. The next section looks at the problems felt by many to be inherent in the case study approach.

Table 6.1: Case studies: strengths and weaknesses

Strengths Case studies should be ...	Weaknesses Case studies may not be ...
illustrative	generalizable
illuminating/insightful	representative
disseminable, accessible	typical
attention-holding	replicable
strong on reality, vivid	repeatable
of value in teaching	

FACING THE PROBLEMS IN CASE STUDY

Three Perennial Problems

The problem of interpretation of data from the study of cases has been discussed briefly in relation to Stenhouse's concern for public verification. The use of case study is problematic for other reasons and three (which are interconnected) are discussed below: generalizability, validity and sampling.

The problem of generalizing from a study of one case is summed up by Bogdan and Biklen (1982):

> Purposely choosing the unusual or just falling into a study leaves the question of generalisability up in the air. Where does the setting fit in the spectrum of human events? The question is not answered by the selection itself, but has to be explored as part of

the study. The researcher has to determine what it is he or she is studying: that is, of what is this a case?

Woods (1986, p. 48) discusses the problem from a different approach – the issue of validity – by suggesting that the problem is not confined only to qualitative (in his case ethnographic) studies:

> Accounts emerging from participant observation work are often accused of being impressionistic, subjective, biased and idiosyncratic. Interestingly ... much so-called 'hard data' is suspect in that often statistical accounts have been accepted as data without seeking to uncover the criteria and processes involved in their compilation.

It is unfair therefore to suggest that a search for validity is a concern only in qualitative research. Nevertheless, two questions do need to be asked of case study research: Is it *externally* valid, or generalizable? Is it *internally* valid? Woods phrases the latter question in the following way: 'Is what we discover the genuine product, and not tainted by our presence or instrumentation?' This problem is as great for research in physics (see Capra, F., 1983) as it is for case study. Instrumentation will always affect the phenomenon under observation, whether at subatomic or human level. It is a feature inherent in any research of any kind which needs to be acknowledged and, most importantly, reflected upon. How does the observer affect the case being studied? To what extent are a researcher's observations and subsequently interpretations theory or value laden? Both questions need to feature prominently in a reflective (or 'reflexive', see Hammersley and Atkinson, 1983) approach to qualitative or indeed quantitative study.

The problem of external validity is related to the issue of sampling. By systematic and purposive sampling a number of cases can be studied which enable valid generalizations to be made. In the case of schools, for example, Woods (1986, p. 49) suggests that

> We can take an area of special interest, say a curriculum innovation, and carry out intensive studies of it within several schools; then, as the study reveals certain particular aspects of interest concerning the innovation, widen the sample of schools.

Responses to the Problem of Generalizability
There have been several interesting responses to this issue, some of them quite ebullient. We consider a few of them below:

- Wolcott (1995, p. 17) is perhaps the most 'bullish' in responding, by posing a question and giving an answer: 'What can we learn from studying only one of anything?' The answer: 'All we can.' He later elaborates on this by arguing that 'Each case study is unique, but not so unique that we cannot learn from it and apply its lessons more generally' (p. 175).

- A similar point was made over 50 years ago by Kluckhohn and Murray (1948, p. 35) in, despite the gendered language, a memorable quote: 'Every man is in certain respects, like all men, like some men, like no other man.' We could add to this: In some ways all schools are the same, in other respects they are all different; similarly for colleges, universities and employers.

- Walker (1980, p. 34) expressed the same view by saying: 'An instance is likely to be as typical and as atypical as any other.'

- Yin (1994) takes a different tack in his book by advocating the use of *multiple case studies*, over an extended period at different sites. These multiple cases can then, *cumulatively*, be used to produce generalizations.

- Finally, Mitchell (1983) argued that, even if case study research cannot produce or create generalizations, it can be used to *explore* them. Thus the study of a case can be valuable in exploring how general principles are exemplified in practice. The study of several cases can be used to gauge the value or extent of a generalization by actively searching for exceptions to it.

Whatever stance we take on the issue of generalizability, there seems to be one important general point. In examining case studies, a large part of the onus rests upon the *reader*. The validity of a study needs to be assessed and judged by the reader, given his or her experience, knowledge and wisdom, i.e. the value, or 'truth', of case study research is a function of the reader as much as the researcher. But this has one important caveat, as Roberts (1996, p. 147) points out: 'As with any research, the reader has to rely on the integrity of the researcher to select and present the evidence fairly.'

Despite the inherent difficulties discussed above in relation to case study research (which are also problems for other forms of research), the study of cases is surely a valuable tool. Its inherent dangers need to be recognized and acknowledged. This can be achieved by a reflective approach and the degree of 'openness' essential in allowing interpretation to be critically examined. Case study can then be rich, interesting and possess wide appeal:

One important advantage of a study of cases is that the richness of the material facilitates multiple interpretations by allowing the reader to use his own experiences to evaluate the data. The research serves multiple audiences. (Roizen and Jepson, 1985)

People reading case studies can often relate to them, even if they cannot always generalize from them.

CASE STUDY RESEARCH: A SUMMARY

This chapter has discussed the main issues and problems in case study research. The short summary below highlights some of the main points worth noting:

Some key features of case study research are that it:

- may involve a wide range of different methodologies;
- is concerned with how things happen and why;
- does not attempt to control events or intervene.

However, there are certain necessary steps which need to be taken:

- define what the case is and what is the 'unit of analysis', e.g. a school, a pupil, a family;
- decide why you have chosen that case, e.g. for an interesting feature, an outstanding achievement;
- identify key informants who are part of the case, e.g. pupils, teachers, perhaps non-teaching staff;
- be aware of the many requirements for carrying out a good case study placed on the researcher:

    A case study is difficult to do well so the researcher contemplating a case study should be experienced in all the requisite separate methods. He or she should have a deep understanding of the relevant literature, be a good question-asker, listener and observer, be adaptable, flexible and have an inquiring and unbiased mind. (Anderson, G., 1990)

7

Survey research

The concern of many participants in, and perhaps readers of, research involving solely in-depth interviews and case studies is that of representativeness. As Bell (1993, p. 8) points out in her introductory guide to potential researchers:

> in case studies, critics point to the problem of representativeness. If the researcher is studying one group in depth over a period of time, who is to say that group is typical of other groups which may have the same title?

One way of allaying such fears has been to add the use of a survey, most commonly involving the use of a questionnaire, to give a 'wider picture' or an overview. This section discusses briefly the use of surveys, their drawbacks and their 'rapid' way of obtaining information, although that information may often be of a rather superficial kind:

> Surveys can provide answers to the questions What? Where? When? and How?, but it is not so easy to find out Why? Causal relationships can rarely if ever be proved by survey method. The main emphasis is on fact-finding. (*Ibid.*, p. 9)

It is probably true that a survey is essentially a fact-finding mission, and may contribute little to developing a hypothesis or shaping theory. However, survey results can be used to test a hypothesis or add weight to a theory. In addition, it is often forgotten that some of the data collected in a survey can be 'qualitative' in nature, e.g. people's views or perceptions of an issue. This data may contribute to the development of theory as much as interview or observational data.

Walker (1985a, p. 91) sums up both the pros and cons of a survey by questionnaire:

The questionnaire is like interviewing-by-numbers, and like painting-by-numbers it suffers some of the same problems of mass production and lack of interpretative opportunity. On the other hand it offers considerable advantages in administration – it presents an even stimulus, potentially to large numbers of people simultaneously, and provides the investigator with an easy (relatively easy) accumulation of data.

SAMPLING AND RESPONSE

One of the key issues in using a survey involves sampling (see Chapter 4). It may not always be possible to decide on a population, let alone survey a sample of it. For example, it might be decided to make a survey of employers' skill needs in the field of new technology, or perhaps of information technology (as in Wellington, 1989). But an attempt to delineate the population will be faced with two major problems, one of definition and the other of finding suitable information. First, what is to count as 'an employer in the field of new technology' (*ibid.*) Secondly, even if criteria could be agreed upon, how is the information on employers to be obtained against which those criteria could be applied? Help in categorizing employers can be obtained from the Standard Industrial Classification (SIC, 1980) but this is now showing signs of datedness. Help in finding names, addresses and information on employers is available from certain directories (e.g. *The Times* 1000; *Key British Enterprises*; Kompass on-line database) but this information may be dated and incomplete (for example, most directories of employing organizations will be heavily loaded towards larger employers).

In short, decisions on sampling are difficult to make without an adequate view of, and information on, the full population from which the sample is taken. Ultimately some sort of 'directory' or list has to be chosen, and its limitations acknowledged. Given this choice, sampling decisions then follow. Sampling might be random. On the other hand, a definite decision might be made to stratify the sample according to certain criteria, e.g. size, region.

The problem of representativeness can therefore be as acute for survey method as it is in case study or interviewing, although many would argue that it can be overcome by appropriate and careful sampling. Unfortunately, such care can be ruined either by a low or an unrepresentative response rate. One stratum of a carefully stratified sample may respond at a far greater rate than another. How will this bias results? An even response rate across all strata of a sample is unlikely to be achieved. Response rate can be improved by care in design, presentation and distribution – these are issues which are discussed shortly.

As an initial summary, Box 7.1 suggests six ways of maximizing response rate in survey research.

Box 7.1: Ways of maximizing response rate

- Target the respondent by name
- Give clear instructions and the usual assurances, e.g. anonymity
- Go for brevity and clarity
- Warn the respondent in advance of its advent
- Include a stamped addressed envelope
- Give polite reminders (after a suitable time) by letter and by phone

And don't take it personally if your response rate is low; it won't be the first time.

METHODS OF DISTRIBUTION

Traditionally, the method used for carrying out a large-scale survey has involved the conventional postal system to distribute question-naires, give polite reminders and receive responses. However, the advent of electronic networks has opened up new possibilities which have yet to be fully exploited in research surveys. Several networks exist which could potentially be more efficient and far quicker in distributing and 'collecting' a questionnaire than by conventional post. The possibility of sending a polite reminder by electronic mail is also present. Large numbers of 'electronic' questionnaires can be distributed via telephone lines from one computer to another – the questionnaire can then be printed out at the receiving end for completion and return by conventional methods, or completed on screen and relayed back over the network.

Electronic distribution of this kind may offer advantages of speed, efficiency and novelty; however, its problems must also be recognized. First, it does raise difficulties over sampling. Those responding are a self-selected sample and are not likely to be representative of the population as a whole, particularly in their use of information technology. Secondly, networks of this kind are, in an important sense, 'closed user groups'. This implies that members of the group use a network (and pay fees for it) to communicate important information among themselves. This adds to their unrepresentative-ness and also means that few will welcome unsolicited mail. Conse-quently, they might respond negatively to a survey. Finally, the responses may be unreflective of the group as a whole. Although this is a problem for a conventional survey it may be even greater with electronic distribution.

In summary then, electronic distribution of a questionnaire is now an important possibility although its limitations such as restricted sampling and biased response need to be acknowledged. It could offer an alternative or, perhaps more safely, an adjunct to conventional post.

QUESTIONNAIRE DESIGN AND CONSTRUCTION

A great deal has been written on the actual design of questionnaires. Valuable summaries for practitioners are provided in Youngman (1986), Cohen and Manion (1994) or Fink (1995). Perhaps the most important point for a questionnaire is that it should begin with straightforward, closed questions, leaving the open-ended, 'matter of opinion' questions to the end. As Neuman (1994, p. 237) put it, 'one should sequence questions to minimize the discomfort and confusion of respondents'. If a questionnaire is broken down into sections, topics or themes, then each section/area of enquiry should follow this pattern, i.e. closed, matter-of-fact questions to begin, followed by the open-ended questions requiring opinions, feelings and value judgements at the end. These can be time-consuming and difficult to answer – and hard to analyse – so it is best to avoid too many. But they will yield fascinating qualitative data.

Phrasing questions in both interviews (see Chapter 5) and questionnaires is a difficult art. Box 7.2 offers some general guidelines.

Secondly, the questionnaire should be targeted at a particular person within a school or other organization. If a range of information is required then a person in a position to co-ordinate and collate that information should be chosen, e.g. a head of department or head of year.

A third simple but important point concerns presentation. Your would-be respondent is likely to receive a fair quantity of unsolicited mail, much of which is filed in the wastepaper bin. If a questionnaire is not attractively and clearly presented, and brief, it may well be ignored. Similarly, a questionnaire sent to a particular person by name is more likely to receive attention than one addressed to 'The Head Teacher', or, worse still, to an organization generally. However, if sampling is done systematically, e.g. a random sample, it may well be impossible to direct questionnaires to particular people. Response rate will, probably, therefore be reduced.

Box 7.2: A few rules on asking questions

- Beware of hypothetical questions, e.g. 'If you were Principal of this college, how would you . . .?'
- Always avoid leading questions, e.g. 'Do you think that all headteachers are incompetent managers?'
- Avoid, or unpack, compound questions (double- or triple-barrelled), e.g. 'When you assess written work do you judge spelling and punctuation and grammar?'
- Avoid 'clever' questions assuming esoteric knowledge, e.g. 'Do you prefer Piaget's or Vygotsky's views on learning?'
- Don't ask questions which are impossible to answer, e.g. 'How much time did you spend on preparing lessons/lectures in the last academic year?'
- Avoid emotive or openly biased language, e.g. 'Do you think that Ofsted inspectors are a bunch of opinionated, right-wing dinosaurs dressed in pin-stripe suits?'
- Beware of ambiguous, unclear, confusing, imprecise or over-general questions, e.g. 'Do you feel that your pupils are not conceptually ready for the National Curriculum?'

There is a delicate balance between strategies for achieving rigorous sampling and tactics for increasing response rate, e.g. by using known contacts.

The design of a questionnaire within a given project should also be influenced by other methods within that project, e.g. an interview schedule, information gathered or issues raised by a case study. This is surely an important feature of triangulation, mentioned earlier. Thus questions which were particularly successful during interview (including open-ended questions) can be followed up with greater numbers of subjects. Interviewing will also help with the wording of questions which should of course be clear and unambiguous. A postal survey not interactive, as an interview is; therefore ambiguity, confusion or sheer lack of communication must be removed before the event rather than during it.

A questionnaire, and the questions within it, can be developed from prior research methods, but the use of a pilot is still essential. The printed word raises problems unforeseen in spoken, human contact. A pilot questionnaire is therefore an essential stage in design and construction. You should not underestimate the amount of time and drafting required to produce a good questionnaire. A pilot questionnaire, in itself, may be version number ten, and the final version may be version number twenty. Testing it on colleagues, friends and family at every stage is one good way to ensure comprehensibility.

A consideration of the analysis of responses must also be a feature of questionnaire design. How is the data collected to be analysed? Will the questionnaire gather masses of information which cannot be categorized or presented in a final report? While drafting the questionnaire you should keep in mind the analysis of the data, and if, for example, you are going to use a computer package such as SPSS (see below), this should influence design of items to ensure ease of data and analysis recording.

Box 7.3: Some guidelines on questionnaire design and layout

- Write a brief covering letter explaining the purpose of the questionnaire and full assurances of confidentiality.
- Give clear instructions on how to fill it in.
- Present it attractively with a clear layout, obvious structure and adequate space for open-ended responses.
- Make the typeface legible and the English readable.
- Don't go over the top with different typefaces, fonts, headings, bold, italics, colour, etc.
- Sequence questions carefully, starting with the easier, closed questions leading up to more thought-provoking, introspective open questions.
- Provide an 'Open Forum' at the end, allowing space for the respondent to say anything they wish to, i.e. a platform or a dais.
- Say 'thank you' at the end.
- Always try it out before distributing to your sample, i.e. *pilot* the questions.

ANALYSING DATA FROM A SURVEY

The use of a survey is often associated with the collection of *quantitative* data. The analysis of such data is often straightforward, given the design of a clear and unambiguous question. Analysis of numerical data can be quicker and greatly enhanced by the use of a computer package such as SPSS (see Youngman, 1986). Unfortunately, a discussion of the many techniques of data analysis of this kind is beyond the scope of this book (see Robson, 1993, ch. 11 as a good starting point and a lead in to the extensive literature on quantitative data analysis).

However, questionnaires can also be of value in collecting *qualitative* data through open-ended questions, e.g. concerning a person or an organization's views, opinions or even predictions. Indeed, data of this kind collected by a postal questionnaire may even be richer, perhaps more truthful, than data collected in a face-to-face interview. The respondent may be more articulate in writing or perhaps more willing to divulge views, especially if anonymity is assured. The potential of a suitably designed questionnaire for allowing free, honest and articulate expression should not be underestimated.

Analysis of such data may be less straightforward than the analysis of quantitative data, but some of the principles outlined earlier in the discussions of interview data and of case study material can be usefully applied. For example, responses can be indexed and categorized, in the hope of discerning patterns or even of developing theory, in much the same way as other qualitative data can be reflected upon and interpreted (see Chapter 10). With this approach, the use of postal surveys need not conflict with the 'humanistic methodology' espoused by Stenhouse and discussed by commentators on that tradition such as Skilbeck (1983) and Rudduck (1985). Moreover, in reporting research, the written opinions and views of, for example, pupils, students, teachers or employers can often enrich a report by providing an authenticity and vividness which tables of figures seldom can.

8

Documentary research

Discussions of the use of documents in the standard methodological literature are sparse and patchy. (Platt, 1981a, p. 31)

Jennifer Platt made this statement in her seminal article on documentary research in the early 1980s. Her remark is still largely true, particularly in the field of educational research. This chapter attempts to consider the literature that is available in this field (drawing particularly on Platt, 1981a; Codd, 1988 and Scott, 1990), and offers classifications and practical suggestions for working in this area of educational research.

WHAT IS DOCUMENTARY RESEARCH?

If we look at the range of methods available to practitioners in educational research we can divide them crudely into those acting as *primary* sources of data and those acting as *secondary* sources. This crude distinction is shown in Figure 8.1. Primary sources would include observation, interviews, questionnaires, focus groups and so on. The secondary sources we will lump together and call 'documents'. For simplicity we will include diaries in this category, though it could be argued that in some research projects these are better regarded as primary sources of data in that they are elicited or initiated by the researcher (discussed below, p. 118).

A list, in no particular order, of documents which can act as valuable sources in educational research might include:

Letters	Annual reports
Minutes of meetings, e.g.	Syllabuses
departmental, whole staff,	Examination papers
governors	Schemes of work
Prospectuses, e.g. school, college	Lesson plans

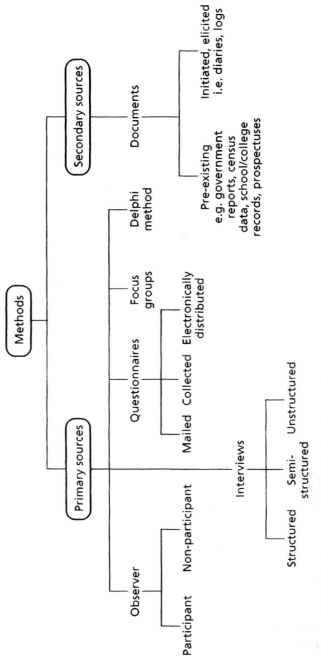

Figure 8.1: Methods of data collection in educational research

Curriculum documents	Web pages
Photographs	Internet material
Audio-tapes	E-mail discussions
E-mail correspondence	Media coverage of education
Inspectors' reports	Circulars
Bulletins to staff	Life histories
Newsletters	Leaflets
Accounts	Video-tape/film
Government papers	Oral histories
Policy documents	Memoirs/autobiographies

The list could include many more: some on paper, some distributed and presented electronically, some on tape or disk. The word 'document' would normally be stretched to include a range of media and modes of presentation.

The use and analysis of documents might be the main focus of a piece of educational research, i.e. the documents are the subject of systematic research in their own right. They are treated as social products and therefore the object of analysis. On the other hand, the study of documents might be done in conjunction with other methods of research, involving primary sources. For example, the collection and analysis of a range of documents will often be done in a case study in conjunction with interviews, observations or questionnaires.

Thus documentary analysis can be the main focus or an adjunct in educational research. Whether the study and analysis of documents is *central* or *complementary*, the discussions below on typology, ethics and methods of analysis all apply equally.

A TYPOLOGY OF DOCUMENTS IN EDUCATIONAL RESEARCH

The jumbled list above shows that 'documents' for educational research might be paper sources, electronic sources, visual sources or aural sources. These may be some of the ways of classifying them but the labels are probably more glib than helpful.

Scott (1990, pp. 12–18) provides a valuable discussion of various types of documents that may form the subject of social research. He suggests a classification according to two different dimensions: access and authorship. Based on Scott's discussion, I put forward a typology of documents for educational research in terms of two different axes, as shown in Figure 8.2.

The vertical axis shows the degree of access or 'openness'. This

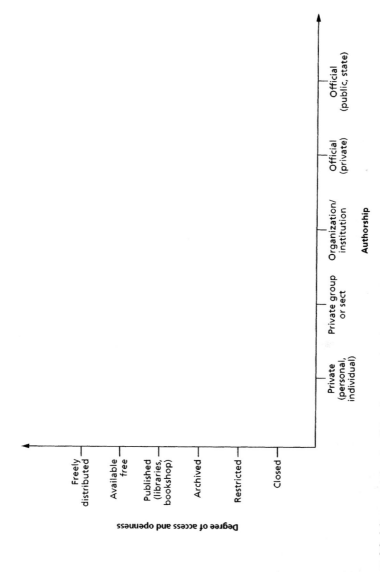

Figure 8.2: A framework for classifying documents in educational research.
Source: After Scott, J., 1990, p. 15

Table 8.1: Examples of different types of documents

Degree of access	Examples
Closed	Available only to a limited number of insiders, e.g. personal diaries, learning logs, letters, school accounts
Restricted	Available only by gaining special permission or having access granted
Archived	Access via a special place of storage, or archive, e.g. very old documents; privately owned papers
Published 1	Available in libraries, bookshops or on the Internet but at a price, e.g. intentionally published diaries, newspapers, White Papers
Published 2	Available free on application or via the Internet, e.g. some government documents, curriculum statements, school or college prospectuses
Published 3	Freely distributed to every household, school, college etc., e.g. health education leaflets, propaganda, pressure group publications

ranges from closed or restricted access to openly published documents and, at the upper end, documents which are not only public but also freely distributed to all. The range of types along this axis, with some examples, is shown in Table 8.1.

Documents for educational research might be positioned anywhere along this continuum. Equally, documents will range along the horizontal axis according to their authorship. This can vary from a private individual to a private group, an organization such as a school, an official private group or to an official, 'public' organization such as a government department. This axis is independent of the vertical axis, i.e. access does not depend on authorship, and vice versa. For example, a document written by a private individual, e.g. a diarist, may, one day, become available publicly; on the other hand it might remain closed or restricted. Equally, documents from the right-hand side of the authorship axis might be written by an official government organization, but could range from completely closed access through to openly published and freely distributed. In other words, documents of value to educational research could lie anywhere on the two-dimensional plane in Figure 8.2.

The framework can be valuable in several ways to educational researchers embarking on documentary research. A given document can be positioned carefully using the typology. This position will have important implications for analysis, ethics and the eventual writing up of the research. Any of the documents in the earlier list can be considered in terms of this typology, according to their authorship and the degree of access. Their position will influence the way we analyse them in terms of their intention, their source and their meaning (see below). Position will also guide the *ethics* of analysis – certain documents, e.g. personal diaries or learning logs will need to be treated sensitively and confidentially. At the other extreme, public documents such as White Papers or National Curriculum statements might be treated as 'fair game' for harsh critical analysis. This, in turn, will guide the ethics of the writing up of any analysis.

Finally, the two-dimensional typology is useful in considering how the position of a document often changes over time. This usually happens with reference to the vertical axis. For example, a personal diary or 'official' government information might shift from being closed and restricted to eventually becoming available publicly via bookshops or other media. Similarly, old archived material on paper, which is often restricted for its own physical protection, might be transcribed onto a CD-ROM or onto the Internet, and thereby made publicly available.

DECIDING ON FOCUS AND APPROACH

As already mentioned, the entire focus of a piece of educational research might be on documents of one kind or another. For example, a historical study might focus on archive material; policy-related research might examine the documents around a certain policy or initiative; research might be library-based or computer-based. But often documentary research is part of a broader approach involving other techniques and methods. The converse is also true; every research project involves, to some extent, the study and analysis of documents, even if this is only done in the literature review.

Plummer (1983, p. 72) suggests that life history approaches can be used at three critical stages in research: the exploratory stage, the complementary stage and the concluding stage. The same idea of stages can be applied in considering when and how to use documents in educational research:

1. The exploratory stage: documents can be used to open up an area of inquiry and sensitize researchers to the key issues and problems in that field. This can be especially useful in an area in which the

problems have not been clearly conceptualized or formulated. Through studying documents, research questions can be articulated or (if this approach is taken) hypotheses can be created. Documents can give researchers a 'feel' for an area:

> Expressive documents have generally been used in the exploratory rather than the final stages of the research process. Their greatest value perhaps has been in giving investigators a feel for the data and thus producing hunches with respect to the most fruitful ways of conceptualising the problem. The research scientist must become intimately familiar with the situation under study, and one of the best ways to do this is with careful readings of insightful expressive documents. (Angell and Freedman, 1953, pp. 305–6)

2. The complementary stage: as well as being of value at the outset of research, documents can enrich a study throughout the research process, i.e. as a complement to other methods and approaches, for example in case study.
3. The concluding stage: Plummer (1983, p. 73) called this the business of 'consolidating, clarifying and concluding'. In Plummer's case life history documents (but more generally any type of document) may be of value in this later stage of evaluating one's own research, clarifying it and considering how it relates to existing published material.

Thus documents can be of value at different stages of research and can be 'brought in' to the research process for different purposes: to open up and explore a field; to complement other research approaches and methods; and to conclude or consolidate research, including the enrichment of the final process of writing up and publishing. The actual business of assessing and analysing documents is discussed in the next section.

ASSESSING DOCUMENTARY SOURCES

Scott (1990, pp. 6–8) suggests four key criteria for assessing the 'quality' of documents:

- *Authenticity*: Is the evidence genuine and of unquestionable origin?
- *Credibility*: Is the evidence free from error and distortion?
- *Representativeness*: Is the evidence typical of its kind and, if not, is the extent of its untypicality known?
- *Meaning*: Is the evidence clear and comprehensible?

These four criteria have *some* applicability to educational research, so are worth considering in more detail. (The origin of these criteria can be found in Platt, 1981a and b.)

First, *authenticity* refers to the origin and the authorship of a document. This criterion would be applied largely in assessing the worth of historical material, e.g. an old diary or a letter, but it could also be used to assess the identity or origin of an interviewee (in some ways this is akin to the idea of validity).

Credibility refers to the extent to which a document (or indeed an interview) is sincere and undistorted. For example, in an interview transcript was the informant taking it seriously? Were they telling 'the truth'? Generally speaking, can a document be taken as a credible, worthwhile piece of evidence? In some cases, is it accurate?

The idea of *representativeness* refers to the 'general problem of assessing the typicality or otherwise of evidence' (Scott, 1990, p. 7). In some ways this relates to the idea of 'generalizability' (just as the first two criteria are related to validity). However, as Scott points out, a researcher does not always want or seek 'typical evidence'. The important skill is to assess how typical or atypical it is before any inferences are drawn (again, this is equally true of any research data). For example, if some old or archived material has survived, e.g. minutes of meetings, lengthy correspondence, and some has not, then how representative is the surviving material?

The final criterion, *meaning*, concerns the assessment of the documents themselves. As Scott puts it: 'What is it and what does it tell us?' (Scott, 1990, p. 8). This is probably the most important and most contentious aspect of documentary research so the next section is devoted to it.

SEARCHING FOR 'MEANING'

This section starts from the premiss, put forward several decades ago, that a text or document does not have a single 'objective' inner, essential meaning. A text is not an 'objective cultural entity' (Giddens, 1976); its meaning depends on the intentions of the author(s) and the perspectives of the reader. To search for a single, objective, essential meaning is to search for a chimera. Texts and documents must be studied and analysed as 'socially situated products' (Scott, 1990, p. 34).

Searching for meaning, therefore, is not some kind of hunt for, or pursuit of, a single inner meaning or essence. It is a matter of interpretation. Documents have multiple meanings. Documentary research starts from the premiss that no document should be accepted at face value, but equally that no amount of analysis will discover or decode a hidden, essentialist meaning. The key activity is one of interpretation rather than a search for, or discovery of, some kind of Holy Grail.

One simple, but useful, distinction is that between *literal* understanding and *interpretative* understanding of a text or document. The former involves the understanding of the literal or surface meaning of the words, terms and phrases – this might be called their denotation. The latter involves a deeper understanding and interpretation of the document – its *connotation*. The activity of exploring and 'decoding' the underlying, hidden meaning of a text is part of the discipline of semiotics (the study of signs and symbols). This is the hermeneutic (interpretative) task in documentary research.

Enough of the jargon: what does this mean when it comes to the practical activity of analysing documents in educational research? It means that the literal reading of a document must be accompanied by an examination of the document's

- context
- authorship
- intended audiences
- intentions and purposes
- vested interests
- genre, style and tone
- presentation and appearance.

These seven points can be used as a framework for exploring and analysing documents of any kind. School prospectuses, government White Papers, minutes of meetings, archived material, staff bulletins, curriculum documents, or indeed any examples from the list on pages 108 and 110, can all be examined using this framework.

Another way of putting it, using postmodernist language, is suggested by Usher and Edwards (1994) and Usher (1996). They suggest four aspects of documents which require interrogation and interpretation:

1. Con-text, e.g. the author's own position;
2. Pre-text – that which exists before the text;
3. Sub-text – that which is beneath the text;
4. Inter-text – the relation of this text to other texts.

My own framework for interrogating documents in educational research is couched in slightly cruder language. In Box 8.1 I suggest eight different areas for interpretation and analysis with a list of questions within each area. Not all of these questions will apply to every document of course but it does provide a useful checklist.

Box 8.1: Questions which might be posed in analysing documents

- *Authorship*: Who wrote it? Who are they? What is their position and their bias?
- *Audience*: Who was it written for? Why them? What assumptions does it make, including assumptions about its audience?
- *Production*: Where was it produced and when? By whom? What were the social, political and cultural conditions in which it was produced?
- *Presentation, appearance, image*: How is it presented, e.g. colour or black and white; glossy paper; highly illustrated? What 'image' does it portray?
- *Intentions*: Why was it written? With what purpose in mind?
- *Style, function, genre*: In what style is it written? How direct is the language? Is it written to inform, to persuade, to convince, to sell, to cajole, to provoke . . .? How clever is the language?
- *Content*: Which words, terms or buzzwords are commonly used? Can their frequency be analysed quantitatively (content analysis)? What rhetoric is used? Are values conveyed, explicitly or implicitly? What metaphors and analogies does it contain? What is *not* in it?
- *Context/frame of reference*: When was it written? What came before it and after it? How does it relate to previous documents and later ones?

Applying this range of questions in the eight areas above involves the researcher in relating his or her background, position and theoretical stance to the position of the document and its authors. As Scott (1990, p. 31) puts it, the business of analysis involves relating the 'frame of reference' of the researcher to that of the document's authors in a kind of dialogue:

> Textual analysis involves mediation between the frames of reference of the researcher and those who produced the text. The aim of this dialogue is to move within the 'hermeneutic circle' in which we comprehend a text by understanding the *frame of reference* from which it was produced, and appreciate that frame of reference by understanding the text. The researcher's own frame of reference becomes the springboard from which the circle is entered, and so the circle reaches back to encompass the dialogue between the researcher and the text.

DIARIES WITH A PURPOSE

The chapter so far has considered the wide range of documents available to researchers: letters, memos, government publications, minutes of meetings, prospectuses and so on. In a sense, all these documents are *pre-existing*, i.e. already there and already written. The researcher's job is one of gaining access to them (if possible) and analysing them as a source of data.

The subject of this section is the diary which is *initiated* by the researcher. This diary is kept by those being researched, the 'informants', with the aim of contributing to or enriching the study. The diary provides an additional source of documentary data which can explore the experiences, activities, thoughts, behaviour and perceptions of informants. It gives their version of events.

This section explores reasons for using diaries, what they might contain, ways of motivating would-be diarists and problems inherent in the use of initiated diaries as a research method.

Why Use Diaries?

As discussed elsewhere, observation is a valuable method in educational research. But it is both practically impossible (for reasons of time and money) and ethically unacceptable (invasion of privacy, too overbearing) to observe the subjects of a research study at all times. In addition, as Zimmerman and Wieder (1977, p. 480) pointed out in a seminal article on the diary as a research method, observation can often be spread out, unpredictable and haphazard. This might be particularly true in studying some settings: learning at home, for example, or within non-formal organizations:

> If the social scene is more diffuse, as within a counter-culture community, the patterns of behaviour in question may have a less precise definition and lack as well the luxury of an eight-to-five work day. Clearly, the less focused the activity, the wider the range of observations required.

For these reasons, diaries can be an excellent additional source of data and provide the informants' own versions or interpretations of events (in either informal or formal educational settings).

What Could Be in a Diary? The Diary Format

A diary is a kind of annotated chronological record or a 'log' of experiences and events (in some ways the use of diaries is akin to the life history approach: Plummer, 1983; Atkinson, 1998). Zimmerman and Wieder (1977, p. 486) give an example where they asked participants for a record of their 'activities' over a period of seven days using the format: Who, What, When, Where, How? The formula may work in some situations, but my view is that in an educational research project informants will need to be asked to focus on certain kinds of activities over a time period, e.g. a learner's use of the Internet in his/her studies over a four-week period. The format required will then depend on the activity focused upon and the researcher's own research questions (as will the time span, e.g. one week, one month, one term, one semester . . .).

No general formula will fit all educational research projects. Perhaps the only general rule is that the researcher requires a chronological account of events with the diarist's own interpretation or version of them, and reflection upon them. One approach is to ask the diarist to look out for, and record, critical events in their experiences, e.g. learning experiences which really 'stick in their minds'. By recording critical or significant incidents (e.g. turning points) the diarist can often convey far more than could be achieved by a daily, blow-by-blow account.

Problems with Diaries as a Source of Data
Problems with diaries can be divided into three areas: practical, ethical and methodological:

- The practical problems of actually getting informants to keep a diary consistently and reliably over a period of time (even one week) should not be underestimated. Keeping a diary is extremely time-consuming and mentally demanding. It also depends on an informant's literary skills, i.e. ability and willingness to write. This may well deter many potential informants and thereby bias a sample.
- One of the ethical problems concerns the amount of time and self-discipline which a researcher is demanding (often free of charge) from the diary keeper. A second problem concerns ownership. Who actually owns the diary? Can a researcher have unlimited access to it? How will personal, confidential information be published in the final report or article? These are all sensitive issues which need careful negotiation, preferably at the start of the research.
- Finally, there are methodological problems (as with every method in research). As already noted, the implicit demand that diarists must be able and willing to write will lead to bias in the data from

this source, i.e. away from those who may be less literate or more oral (unless the diary is recorded onto audio tape).

In addition, the diary, as with every research method, has an effect on the subject of the research. As Oppenheim (1966, p. 215) put it:

> the respondent's interest in filling up the diary will cause him to modify the very behaviour we wish him to record. If, for instance, he is completing a week's diary of his television-viewing behaviour, this may cause him to engage in 'duty viewing' in order to 'have something to record', or he may view 'better' types of programmes in order to create a more favourable impression.

This effect must be recognized both in analysing and in writing-up the research.

Motivating the Diarist

One of the main difficulties with diaries as a research method is to persuade the diarist to maintain it conscientiously and consistently over an extended time period, i.e. more than one week. One solution is to pay them for their efforts. Zimmerman and Wieder reported a payment of $10 (in 1977) for a 'reasonably conscientious effort'. This may be money well spent.

A less mercenary approach is to persuade the diarists of their importance in helping with worthwhile research, i.e. to gain support and sympathy for the cause. In addition, at the start of the diary-keeping, researchers can check the diarist's progress and answer any questions he might have. During the course of the recording, researchers will also need to monitor progress, make encouraging noises and generally chivvy him along. Finally, of course, diarists need to be thanked profusely, especially if they have maintained a diary for four weeks or more.

Diaries then are not without their practical, methodological and ethical problems. But they can be a valuable alternative way of gathering data and triangulating. They can provide a rich complement to, say, interviewing and observation. Indeed, in some ways they are better than both, especially suited to those who prefer to write their thoughts and perceptions (in their own good time) as opposed to being questioned orally or observed *in situ*.

The Diary Diary-Interview Method

Diaries can be a valuable and interesting research method in themselves. But it is worth noting briefly here that several writers see their main worth as the precursor to in-depth interviews. The statements made by the diarist are then used 'as a way of generating questions for the subsequent diary interview' (Zimmerman and Wieder, 1977, p. 489). According to these authors the purpose of the follow-up interview is to allow *expansion*, i.e. filling in missing details, and further *exploration*, i.e. probing more deeply into the diarist's attitudes, experiences and beliefs.

IN SUMMARY

This chapter has considered a large range of documentary sources and their potential for educational research. Some of these sources are *pre-existing*; others are *initiated*, elicited and sometimes sponsored by the researcher, i.e. the research diary.

As with all methods in educational research, the business of collecting and analysing documentary data is accompanied by the usual issues of access, ethics and researcher effect. But the use of documentary sources has a number of advantages in any research project on education:

- they can provide an important historical perspective on any area of education;
- documents provide an excellent source of additional data, e.g. as a complement to interviews or observation (especially suited to some respondents);
- documentary research can be extremely efficient, cost-effective and productive;
- it forms an excellent means of triangulation, helping to increase the 'trustworthiness', reliability and validity of research (especially as most documents are publicly accessible).

9

Two other methods

This short chapter considers two methods which can be used to enrich both case-study and survey research.

THE DELPHI METHOD

The first method worth mentioning, which has been used in several contexts to collect both quantitative and qualitative data, has been named the Delphi Method. It was developed by Olaf Helmer in connection with the analysis of military strategies and technological innovation (Helmer, 1972). As its name suggests, the Delphi method makes use of expert opinions to produce 'oracular statements' regarding the likelihood of future events taking place. The essential features of the Delphi method are summed up by Helmer (1972, p. 15) as follows:

> Delphi is a systematic method of collecting opinions from a group of experts through a series of questionnaires, in which feedback of the group's opinion distribution is provided between question rounds while preserving the anonymity of the responses.

There are three main components in the Delphi method: the creation of a panel of experts who can be consulted, the use of a series of questionnaires for consultation purposes and the provision that is made for the feedback of findings to respondents:

1. A common feature of all applications of the Delphi method is the use of a group or panel of experts. The criteria for the selection of these experts varies according to the application that is envisaged. Generally, experts are selected for their knowledge of the area and problems that are being considered. In most cases the research co-ordinator will seek to create a panel that reflects a wide range of

experience and a diversity of opinions on the subjects that are being considered.

2. The second common element in Delphi applications is the use of a series of questionnaires to obtain the necessary responses. Most Delphi applications involve several rounds of questionnaires. Generally, a broad range of topics is examined in the first round and open-ended questions may also be included to explore the personal reactions of the participants. In later rounds, however, a more limited range of topics is usually explored in a more structured way. The nature of the questions that are asked will vary from study to study.

3. The third element in Delphi applications is the use that is made of feedback procedures to develop and extend the analysis of the responses to the questionnaires. The analysis of results is usually presented in such a way that the entire range of responses can be seen by the participants. Findings can then be utilized in two main ways. First, they may be sent to respondents with an invitation to them to revise their initial predictions if they wish. The aim of such an exercise is to see whether there is a tendency towards a convergence of opinion once the views of other respondents are known. With this in mind, respondents taking up extreme positions relative to the group are likely to be asked by the organizers to give reasons for their non-conforming opinions. Secondly, the findings of one round of questionnaires may be used to develop a new questionnaire which is administered either to the initial group or a modified panel of respondents.

Helmer's description also draws attention to the extent to which the Delphi method preserves the anonymity of the respondents. This is very important in many applications as it enables participants to revise their views without publicly admitting that they have done so. It also encourages participants to take up a more personal viewpoint rather than the relatively cautious institutional position that they may feel obliged to adopt in public (see, for example, Dickey and Watts, 1978, p. 217).

The main strengths of the Delphi method lie in the way that it utilizes expert opinion to produce forecasts and the wide range of interrelated variables that can be taken account of in the process. Because of the emphasis that it gives to tangible outputs rather than the detailed technical analysis that is often required to produce them, the Delphi method is also a useful device for communicating with groups representing a range of professional and lay interests. Finally, from the standpoint of the researcher, the method has the advantage of being relatively inexpensive to organize and administer, provided a panel of experts can be assembled who are willing to give time to the project.

The practical benefits of the Delphi method have been widely recognized and there have been a very large number of applications over a wide range of fields. Perhaps its main strength lies in forecasting the future, e.g. in making predictions about future trends in education, skill needs and skill shortages, although even the use of selected 'experts' could never confer any certainty on those predictions or forecasts.

The Delphi method is vulnerable to charges that it operates without theory and that its protocols are designed to produce consensus irrespective of historical truth (Fowles, 1976, p. 260). It also shares the disadvantages of most procedures that seek to make use of expert opinions. Because of this, critics such as Sackman (1976, p. 446) argue that there is a need to examine expert behaviour in much more detail before any measure of confidence can be placed in studies of this kind.

FOCUS GROUPS

A final and rather similar method which can enrich and complement both survey research, or a case study, involves the use of 'focus groups'. Focus groups are often seen as best for giving insights of an exploratory or preliminary kind (Krueger, 1994). But they can also be a stand-alone, self-contained way of collecting data for a research project, i.e. as a primary method (Morgan, 1988, p. 10).

What Is a Focus Group?

A focus group is a small group made up of perhaps six to ten individuals with certain common features or characteristics, with whom a discussion can be focused onto a given issue or topic. For example, it might be a group of teachers, a sample of employers in a particular sector of industry, a group of pupils/students or a selection of headteachers. It is often a homogeneous group of people. Groups might meet perhaps three or four times or have as many as a dozen meetings. A group session may last from 45 minutes to two hours.

A focus group is rather more than a group interview. The focus group sets up a situation where the synergy of the group, the interaction of its members, can add to the depth or insight of either an interview or a survey. Quite simply, members of the group, brought together in a suitable, conducive environment, can stimulate or 'spark each other off'.

Examples of Focus Groups

My own experience of using focus groups comes from a project which explored teachers' views of the nature of science and went on to consider the implications of those views for science education (Lakin and Wellington, 1994). Individual teachers were interviewed using a method which Susanne Lakin had adapted from personal construct theory. In addition, we formed two focus groups of teachers to explore their feelings and views about the nature of science and its influence on their teaching. The groups met twice only, due to constraints on their own time, but provided a lot of insight to complement the one-to-one research.

Morgan (1988, pp. 9–10) gives three short examples of other uses of focus groups:

i) In a seminar room, a group of returning students, all in their forties, are discussing the role of stress in causing heart attacks. There is consensus around the table that stress is indeed important, but what matters even more is how one deals with this stress.

ii) In a rural village in Thailand, two groups, one of young men and one of young women, discuss the number of children they want to have and how this has changed since their parents' day.

iii) In a church meeting room, a group of young widows compare their experiences. One woman complains that other people wanted to stop her grieving in six months but that really it takes much longer. Another agrees, and says that in some ways the second year is harder than the first.

Conducting a Focus Group

The focus group needs to be carefully planned and chosen with the objectives of the research in mind. Some agenda needs to be set although (as with interviews) degrees of structure can vary. The group requires a skilled moderator or leader and a convivial setting. Group members need to be at ease, and seated so that all of the group can make eye contact with each other.

Data can be collected with a good quality tape recorder, given the group's permission (a recorder with a poor microphone may be good enough for one-to-one interviews but will not pick up all the voices of a group). Some researchers advocate the use of video recording but this can be off-putting. Detailed notes will also be needed. Ideally, a written account of the meeting(s) should be fed back to group members for comment. Box 9.1 below gives a summary of some of the main points to remember when planning and carrying out focus group work.

Box 9.1: A Checklist for conducting focus group interviews

1. **Planning**
   Contact participants by phone one to two weeks before the session.
   Send each participant a letter of invitation.
   Give the participants a reminder phone call prior to the session.
   Slightly over-recruit the number of participants.
2. **Asking the Questions**
   The introductory question should be answered quickly and not identify status.
   Questions should flow in a logical sequence.
   Key questions should focus on the critical issues of concern.
   Consider probe or follow-up questions.
   Limit the use of 'why' questions.
   Use 'think back' questions as needed.
   Provide a summary of the discussion and invite comments.
3. **Logistics**
   The room should be satisfactory (size, tables, comfort etc.).
   The moderator should arrive early to make necessary changes.
   Background noise should not interfere with the tape recording.
   Microphone should be placed on the table.
   Bring extra tapes, batteries etc.
4. **Moderator Skills**
   Be well rested and alert for the focus group session.
   Ask questions with minimal reference to notes.
   Be careful to avoid head-nodding.
   Avoid comments that signal approval, such as 'Excellent', 'Great', 'Wonderful'.
   Avoid giving personal opinions.
5. **Immediately After the Session**
   Prepare a brief written summary of key points as soon as possible.
   Check to see if the tape recorder captured the comments.

Source: Adapted from Krueger, 1994, pp. 122–3

Although they have been most commonly used in private sector market research in the last 30 years, focus groups do have a value in other qualitative research and, indeed, were born in 1930s social science work (Rice, 1931) and were used in the Second World War. Some feel that they may now experience a revival in social science (Krueger, 1994). My own view is that focus groups can be a valuable tool, efficient for collecting data and sometimes giving insights in addition to one-to-one interviews. (For a full account see Anderson, G. (1990) pp. 241–8, Krueger (1994) for a whole book on focus groups and Morgan (1988) for a shorter guide.) Box 9.2 gives a summary of the main features, advantages and disadvantages of focus groups.

Box 9.2: Key features of focus groups

Researcher's Role: organizer, manager, moderator, facilitator, chair, stimulator, observer.

Data Provided: notes and transcripts of the group's discussion and observations of the participants' interaction and body language.

Emphasis: use of the group interaction to produce data and insights which would not arise without it.

Sampling: participants chosen for their characteristics relating to the topic/research question.

Problems: people not turning up; over-dominant members (maverick voices, long monologues); quiet members; poor meeting places, e.g. cold or noisy rooms; quiet, 'cold' groups or noisy, over-excited, emotional groups.

Ethical Issues: confidentiality; people's feelings on controversial or sensitive subjects; using too much of people's time, or money for travel, i.e. over-exploitation.

Advantages: produces a substantial set of data/observations in a short time; quicker and cheaper than a series of one-to-one interviews; can be a more natural environment than a one-to-one interview; the group itself may 'progress' as a result of its involvement in the research.

Disadvantages: unnatural social settings, e.g. a hotel room, a seminar room, someone's house; less researcher control than in one-to-one interviews.

Main Strength: the opportunity for creating and collecting data resulting from group interaction.

Concluding remarks on Part 2

Part 2 of the book has examined a variety of methods which might be used in a study. The intricacies of those methods and the care and reflection which should be taken in their use have been discussed in each case. I have argued that researchers should pay careful attention to possible sources of error, whether in interviewing, case study or the use of a questionnaire.

I have tried to illustrate that different methods, supposedly from different traditions, need not be incompatible with each other, and can cut across boundaries such as the qualitative/quantitative distinction. Different methods can provide different insights and answer different questions. Evidence from one mode of inquiry can supplement and be integrated with evidence from another. Yin (1984, p. 84) in his handbook on case study research cites one example in his own study of urban bureaucracies:

> Certain studies may benefit when the same questions are posed for two pools of 'sites' – a smaller pool that is the subject of case studies, and a larger pool that is the subject of a survey. The answers can be compared for consistency, but the case study sites can allow some insight into the causal processes, whereas the survey sites can provide some indication of the prevalence of the phenomenon.

A similar point was made by Faulkner (1982, pp. 80–1) in proposing his notion of a 'Triad', similar of course to the notion of triangulation:

> The strategic strengths and advantages of multi-method inquiry stand on three legs that I have called a Triad. Each leg represents a unique mode of data collection: one from interviews with both informants and respondents; the second from observation of people at work; and the third from documents, records and archives of the organisation or industry in question. Each leg

presents the researcher with a different vantage point. While it may be useful to focus extensive time and energy on one mode, the advantages of moving sequentially across all three are formidable.

Alongside the three legs of Faulkner's triad, of course, can be added the fourth leg of a *survey*, by post, telephone or electronic means.

In a research study the use of a 'triangulation' of methods can overcome some of the problems discussed above. The value of first-hand observation, for example, can be immense in overcoming the 'image presentation' or 'public relations front' which an interviewee from a school or indeed any organization may put forward during a face-to-face interview. The classic problem of whether a key informant is 'telling the truth' (Dean and Whyte, 1969) or merely presenting an image can be overcome partly by interviewing informants at different levels (e.g. workers on the shop floor as well as the personnel manager; students in a school as well as teachers) but also by first-hand observation or informal discussion within the organization. This can be achieved in a case study.

In addition, the opportunity to provide information anonymously in a survey will allow a range of written responses by a greater sample of people to be compared.

Finally, the most valuable aspect of triangulation is its use in *validation* – in validating statements, interview records, transcribed accounts, evidence from case-study or data from a survey. As Woods (1986, p. 87) argues, triangulation can provide both strength and accuracy:

> Triangles possess enormous strength. Among other things, they make the basic frames of bicycles, gates and house roofs. Triangulation enables extraordinary precision over phenomenal distances in astronomy. Similarly, in social scientific research, the use of three or more different methods or bearings to explore an issue greatly increases the chances of accuracy.

But this is too comfortable a note on which to finish. The practicalities of doing real research which does not involve the inanimate objects, idealized entities and high-level abstractions of the physical sciences should not be forgotten – most educational research deals with people and organizations which are far more complex than the 'frictionless objects', 'point masses' and 'rigid bodies' of physics. Things can and will go wrong. People don't always co-operate.

Codes of ethics, such as honesty and sensitivity, have to be obeyed.

Prearranged interviews do not always happen. Hours of observation can sometimes yield very little 'useful' data. Researchers can rarely gain access to the students, schools, teachers or classes they would ideally like to study, or at a time when they can do it. Insiders are usually (quite rightly) wary and suspicious of outsiders studying 'their' organization or behaviour.

Above all, anyone doing educational research needs to be tactful, persistent, polite, socially skilled and in possession of a resilient sense of humour.

Part 3: Analysing and Presenting

—10——————————

Dealing with qualitative data

There are several important features of qualitative research:

1. it is usually an exploratory activity;
2. data is usually collected in a real-life, natural setting and is therefore often rich, descriptive and extensive;
3. the human being or beings involved are the main research 'instrument';
4. the design of a study emerges or evolves 'as you go along' – sometimes leading to a broadening or blurring of focus, at other times leading to a narrowing or sharpening focus;
5. the typical methods used are observation, interview, collection of documents and sometimes photography or video recording.

These features of qualitative research (discussed fully in Maykut and Morehouse, 1994, pp. 43–9) lead to one major consequence: qualitative research produces large amounts of data! The data are lengthy and, by definition, verbose, i.e. mostly in the form of words. This is why, with many researchers using largely qualitative methods, panic commonly sets in: 'I can't see the wood for the trees'; 'What am I going to do with all these data . . . ?'

The problem is multiplied because (in my own experience) the inevitable tendency with data is to *over*-collect and *under*-analyse. For example, people carrying out Masters' theses or other research projects usually tend to collect far too many data, for fear that they won't have enough, and then either run out of time, words or energy when it comes to analysing, interpreting, discussing or 'locating' the data. Few researchers successfully 'milk data for all that they're worth'. One superb exception is Edwards and Mercer's (1993) analysis of 'common knowledge'. From a small number of careful and detailed classroom observations and follow-up interviews they succeed in constructing a high-quality argument about teacher–pupil interactions, the pursuit of 'ground rules' in classroom life and shared meanings. The quality of their work derives not from the quantity of their data but from their interpretation of it and from the connections they make with existing theoretical models, e.g. Vygotskyian.

This chapter offers some ideas and further reading on qualitative data analysis. It starts from the premiss that there is not one, single, correct way of doing it. Quite simply, 'there are many ways of analysing qualitative data' (Coffey and Atkinson, 1996, p. 3). But there are general principles and guidelines which can be followed in doing it systematically and reflectively.

Perhaps the main point is that data analysis is an integral part of the whole research process. It should start early. It is not a separate stage, coming towards the end of a linear research path, i.e. just before writing up (see Chapter 11). Data analysis is part of the research cycle, not a discrete phase near the end of a research plan. It must begin early, in order to influence emerging research design and future data collection, i.e. it is formative, not summative.

STAGES IN DATA ANALYSIS

One of the really valuable and practical guides to qualitative data analysis is Miles and Huberman (1994). They break down the business of analysing data into three stages: data reduction, data display and conclusion drawing and verification.

Data reduction consists of data selection and condensation. In this stage, data are collated, summarized, coded and sorted out into themes, clusters and categories.

Data display is the process they suggest next. Here, data are organized and assembled, then 'displayed' in pictorial, diagrammatic or visual form. This 'display' allows the researcher to conceptualize (get their head around) the data, leading towards interpretation and conclusion drawing.

Conclusion drawing, the third process, involves interpreting and giving meaning to data. This process (discussed below) involves searching for themes, patterns and regularities, and the activity of comparing or contrasting units of data.

These stages provide a useful starting point. In my own experience, the activity of analysing qualitative data is often more messy and complicated than this. To put it crudely, it involves taking all the data in, digesting them, taking them apart, then putting them back together again (leaving lots of bits lying around unused at the end) and sometimes returning to collect more. I suggest the following stages:

1. Immersion

This involves getting an overall sense or feel for the data, e.g. listening to tapes or reading and re-reading transcripts. It involves note taking, active reading, highlighting or annotating transcripts. This is the stage of 'immersing oneself' in the data – which can often give rise to a drowning or sinking feeling to carry the metaphor further!

Essentially it involves hearing what your data have to say to you (Riley, 1990; Rubin and Rubin, 1995).

2. Reflecting

The next stage is often to 'stand back' from the data or, literally, to 'sleep on it'. This is, allegedly, the way in which the nineteenth century chemist Kekulé 'discovered' the structure of Benzene. He struggled in his lab for months to put forward a model or theory which would explain its properties and structure. Then one tired night he fell asleep in front of his hearth and dreamt of snakes curled up around a campfire. Each snake had its tail in another's mouth, completing a stable, cosy and complete ring. Kekulé woke up and, before breakfast, had postulated the theory of the Benzene ring, a major breakthrough in organic chemistry.

This story may take liberties with the truth and Kekulé's sleepy insight did follow months of painstaking research (as Pasteur once said, 'Chance favours the prepared mind'). But it does show the importance of standing back from data which a researcher may be very close to.

3. Taking Apart/Analysing Data

The word 'analyse' literally means to break down into components, or to divide a whole into its parts. This is the stage which is, strictly speaking, the analysis phase.

The activity of taking apart or analysing the data can involve:

(a) Carving it up into manageable 'units' or chunks, e.g. sections of an interview transcript. This can be done by literally using scissors and paste on a photocopy of the transcript, or electronically if the material is on disk.
(b) Selecting or filtering out units which can be used: this process

inevitably depends on the researcher's 'judgement', a term which carries many connotations.

(c) Categorizing or coding units, i.e. beginning to create categories, patterns or recurring themes which can gradually be used to 'make sense' of the data.

(d) Attempting to subsume subsequent units of data under these provisional categories, or, if units do not fit, then developing new categories in which they can find a home (very similar to Piaget's processes of assimilation and accommodation by which children make sense of the world).

By this stage the process of taking apart or dividing up the data is well underway. The next phase, of putting it back together again, is beginning as the categories develop.

4. Recombining/Synthesizing Data

The stages described so far are the first part of the classic *constant comparative method* of analysing qualitative data. A simplified model is shown in Figure 10.1 (Glaser and Strauss, 1967; Lincoln and Guba, 1985). It is sometimes referred to as the method of constant comparison and contrast.

As Delamont (1992) described it, this phase consists of searching for patterns, themes and regularities in the data or units of data; it also involves looking for contrasts, paradoxes and irregularities.

As the categories emerge they can be applied in assimilating new data – or they can be adapted to accommodate other material. The next stage is to examine and refine the categories themselves. Researchers can look for *similar* categories which could then perhaps be merged to form one new one. Conversely, one category might be developing into a large, amorphous class encompassing far too much. It then becomes too big and too unwieldy. The category needs to be divided into two or even three smaller groups.

This examination of the categories themselves is an activity of *continuous refinement*. Early categories are adapted, merged, subdivided or simply omitted: new categories are developed. New patterns and relationships are discovered (discussed in more detail in Maykut and Morehouse, 1994, pp. 134–6; and, more generally, in Goertz and Le Compte, 1981).

The 'carving up', or analysis, stage literally involves cutting them up and taking them out of their context, i.e. *decontextualizing* the data. The re-combining, or synthesis, stage involves *recontextualizing it*; finding them a new home.

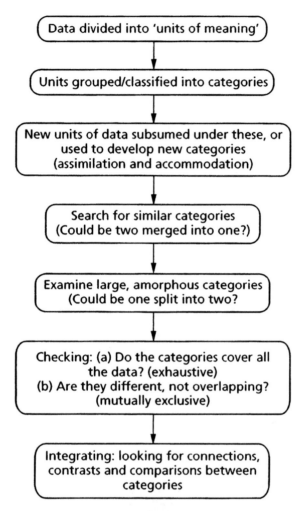

Figure 10.1: The 'Constant Comparative Method' and 'Continuous Refinement' of categories. *Source:* Author's own interpretation, based on Lincoln and Guba (1985), Glaser and Strauss (1967), Goertz and Le Compte (1981)

The next stage is to integrate the data so that they 'hang together' and also to begin to locate one's own data in existing work, i.e. other people's data.

5. Relating and Locating Your Data
Your inquiry, to use a common analogy, is just another brick in the wall. The next stage is therefore to position this brick and relate it to

the existing structure. This important activity can only be done, of course, from a position of knowing and understanding existing research, i.e. from the base of a strong literature review.

The process of locating and relating again involves the use of constant comparison and contrast. This can be used in examining areas: categories, methods and themes.

1. How do your *categories* compare or contrast with others in the literature?
2. What are the strengths and weaknesses of your data and your methods? How do they compare or contrast with the strengths and weaknesses in the methodology of other studies?
3. What theories/frameworks/models have been applied in, or developed from, other inquiries? To what extent can they be applied in yours?

The business of locating and relating your data to other people's research is an important part of reflecting upon it and making sense of it. Having reflected back on it, in some research projects one might see the need to actually return for more data. In some projects this is practical and realistic, i.e. given time and resources. In others, this may not be possible. In many it may not be necessary.

Knowing when to stop.   Whatever the circumstances, we have to stop somewhere. Knowing when to stop collecting data is difficult, but most experienced researchers (to use yet another metaphor) talk of reaching a kind of 'saturation point'. After a certain number of, say, interviews or case studies, perspectives and issues begin to recur and reappear. Interviewees begin to repeat important points; case studies begin to exhibit recurring themes and patterns. This can be very comforting for a researcher and can begin to create some confidence in generalizability. It is a nice feeling; a kind of redundancy in the data eventually develops and the researcher knows that future data collection will be subject to the law of diminishing returns. Categories and themes have begun to develop in the researcher's mind and subsequent data collection serves only to support and reinforce them. This is at once the beauty of doing research – and the danger of knowledge which is constructed by humans. The history of physics and astronomy is riddled with examples. In the context of educational research, Powney and Watts (1987, p. 37) wrote a nice passage on this problem:

> After several (interviews) ... expectations of getting a different

perspective have faded and the presentation of the interviewer may even diminish the chances of the interviewee saying anything different from the previous contributors – or at least the chances of the interviewer recognising original ideas have diminished. This is not laziness or even incompetence but a result of the interviewer's endeavour to build a coherent and total pattern from the responses to the main issues relevant to the inquiry. The interviewer may only hear responses compatible with the picture which is taking shape.

Any observer, researcher or physical scientist needs to be aware of this problem. But in reality most studies do reach a saturation point, when 'newly collected data is redundant with previously collected data' (Maykut and Morehouse, 1994, p. 62). Some qualitative research authors have even (rather ironically) attempted to quantify this point. Lincoln and Guba (1985) suggested that a careful study using emergent sampling can reach saturation point with as few as twelve participants and usually no more than twenty. Douglas (1985) suggested that in-depth interviews with about 25 people were needed before his research reached saturation.

When we begin to experience a situation of diminishing returns from new data collection we can have *some* confidence that (a) the sample size has been adequate (b) our study has been thorough (c) our findings can be discussed and presented with some confidence in their generalizability and 'trustworthiness'. The activity of presenting and disseminating is the next stage.

6. *Presenting Qualitative Data*

The final, and arguably the most important, stage in any research project is to present the data as fairly, clearly, coherently and attractively as possible. Justice needs to be done, and to be seen to be done. In qualitative research, this is where verbatim quotes can come into their own. They can give a research publication (be it a book, thesis, article or a newspaper summary) a reality and vividness which quantitative data cannot.

The problem, of course, is one of how to select these verbatim accounts and 'voices' and how many to use, given the usual constraints on every platform for publication. Should we select only the snappy, glib statements, i.e. the 'sound bites'? On the other hand, should we also use the longer, heartfelt accounts or anecdotes that are sometimes yielded in the best interviews? Should we only look for quotable 'gems' which will enrich and enliven our own perhaps more boring written work ... or should we try to be fair to all our informants?

One thing is certain: difficult choices have to be made. An in-depth interview for 30–40 minutes can be transformed into as much as twelve pages of transcript. Thus the 25 interviewees needed to reach Douglas' (1985) saturation point will produce 300 pages of print. At 250 words per page the interview data alone would amount to about 75,000 words (the size of many PhD theses).

There are no straightforward answers. Choices have to be made and this entails being savage and ruthless. My own view is that verbatim quotes can be used to illustrate and reinforce key themes or perspectives – but it is impossible to represent every 'voice'.

Peter Woods (1999, p. 56) explains the harsh business of filtering and choosing much more eloquently than I can:

> Do you illustrate a point by one lengthy detailed statement, or by smaller extracts from several, or by some combination from the two? I always like to demonstrate the breadth of support for a point and its nature, while including somewhere a lengthier statement if one of quality exists. Then how do you choose the extracts? The simplest answer, again, is by quality, by the telling point, a particularly articulate or expressive section, a striking metaphor. Pressure of space might force you to pare these down to bare essences. You may even have to use précis, paraphrase or reported speech. These techniques allow you to include more and more of the data, but, of course, with each stage you move further from the voice of the other and more towards your own. All we can say is that as far as is possible, the final product should be fair, rigorous, and keep faith with the original meanings.

The more general issue of writing-up research, structuring and presenting work, and attempting to reach different audiences is discussed in the next chapter.

The aim of this section has been to identify and describe the various stages or processes which need to be worked through in making sense of qualitative data. Six stages have been identified as a kind of checklist – these are summarized crudely in Figure 10.2.

This can be a long and sometimes lonely business. One can never be sure if the data have been analysed fairly, adequately or reliably. However, several strategies can assist a researcher in improving the reliability and 'trustworthiness' of these processes: talking over the

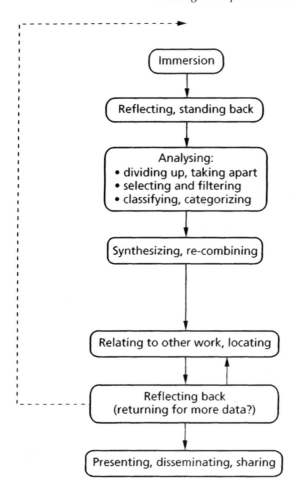

Figure 10.2: General stages in making sense of qualitative data

data and discussing it with others who are complete 'outsiders'; conferring with other researchers if you and they are part of a research team; or presenting the data in an unanalysed form at a seminar or discussion group. These tactics can all be valuable and effective in helping to conceptualise or make sense of qualitative (or quantitative) data.

The next section goes on to look in more detail at specific ways of analysing qualitative data from different sources.

EXACTLY HOW DO WE ANALYSE DATA?

A Priori or A Posteriori Categories?
The first general issue to raise is: Are categories for analysis brought to the data or are they derived from it? Quite simply, there can be three possibilities here:

1. The categories used to analyse the data are *pre-established*, i.e. *a priori*. This can occur if they are derived from the literature, e.g. from a previous research study in this area. Those pre-existing, *a priori* categories which have been used in previous research are then applied to one's own, new data. This can occur, for example, in research attempting to replicate earlier work. The use of *a priori* categories also occurs if a researcher or a research team decide on categories *before* data collection begins for other reasons. For example, they may have been told (in funded research) to explore certain themes or issues, or to investigate certain questions. In another situation, a research or research team may put forward certain hypotheses which then guide data collection and data analysis.

2. The categories used to analyse data are not pre-established but are derived from the data themselves, i.e. *a posteriori*. Categories are then said to 'emerge' from the data by some sort of process of induction. Frankfort-Nachmias and Nachmias (1992, p. 323) describe this 'extraction' as 'inductive coding'.

    The 'emergence' of categories from newly collected data often occurs in a project and this can be one of the more satisfying aspects of doing research. But we should never pretend that they somehow magically or mysteriously do this independently of the researcher like Excalibur rising from the lake. This pretence would be naïve realism or empiricism at its worst. No, the 'emergence' of categories from data depends entirely on the researcher. This is part of the 'research act' (Denzin, 1970). In educational research, as in the physical sciences, theories do not come from observations or experiences; they come from people.

3. The third possibility is that some categories are pre-established while others are derived from the data, i.e. a mixture of *a priori* and *a posteriori*.

    This is probably the most common and, in my view, the most rational approach to analysing qualitative data. In my experience it almost always happens whether people admit it or not.

Existing categories, derived from past research and previous literature, can be brought to the data and used to make sense of it. But frequently there will be new data which require new thought and new categorization (even in a replicative study). Pre-existing categories may not be enough to exhaust all the data and it can feel very unsatisfactory to develop a 'sweeper' category ('miscellaneous') in an attempt to be exhaustive. This is where creativity is required in analysing data and developing new categories in an attempt to consider and do justice to it all. New data can also show that pre-existing categories are not mutually exclusive, i.e. they overlap and data could easily fit into more than one.

In summary, new research can help to refine and clarify existing categories – new research can also help to develop new categories, frameworks and theories.

A Framework for Analysing Interview Responses
Often, in analysing interview data, a researcher is faced with a huge volume of material. When tapes are transcribed onto paper the task looks even more daunting. As mentioned earlier, there is no substitute for initially 'immersing' oneself in the data, i.e. hearing or reading it, and re-hearing or re-reading it, over and over again. Gradually we then begin to make sense of it and begin to categorize and organize it in our own minds.

Unfortunately, there are few published frameworks available which can be of general use in analysing the responses of interviewees. One which does look interesting and widely applicable is derived from the work of Jean Piaget in 1929. (I am grateful to Ruth Jarman of Queen's University in Belfast for bringing this to my attention in her PhD thesis on continuity and progression.)

Piaget (1929) suggested five categories of response which occurred in interviews with children. These can be adapted and extended to form a framework for classifying interviewee's responses in other contexts. Expressed very simply and concisely, the five categories are:

1. **Answers at random**. These occur when the interviewee apparently reveals little or no interest in the topic of the interview. A 'random' answer is given, just to 'move on' or to attempt to satisfy the interviewer.
2. **Suggested conceptions**. Suggested conception is caused by poor interview technique, i.e. by asking questions that suggest the nature of a response, 'leading' questions. As discussed elsewhere, it is difficult to eliminate suggestions completely, although sug-

gestive questions can be minimized by interview practice, and by listening back or reflecting upon previous interviews.

3. **Liberated conceptions**. A liberated conception is a careful response to a question or an issue that is new to the interviewee. This type of response occurs when the interviewee, after reflecting, draws the answer from his or her previous knowledge. Liberated conceptions can therefore be seen as indicative of an interviewee's ideas. Piaget (1929) describes them as original products of the interviewee's mind. Such responses might arise when an interviewee thinks for the first time about an issue or a question posed by the interviewer.

4. **Spontaneous conceptions**. In the mode of liberated conception the interviewee's answer is not spontaneous, but reflected. During this reflection, interviewees consider the knowledge they already possess and construct conceptualizations based on this knowledge and reasoning. Spontaneous conception occurs when an interviewee answers a question straightaway, with no need to reflect. Spontaneous conceptions were already 'set up' before the question was asked: 'There is thus spontaneous conviction when the problem is not new to the child and when the reply is the result of a previous original reflection' (*Ibid.*, p. 11). Thus, spontaneous conception is a response made as a result of previous reflection. It is an immediate response, in that the issue or question is not new to the interviewee.

5. **Romancing**. Romancing occurs when the interviewee invents an answer that he or she does not believe in. In this case the interviewee is simply 'playing a game'. Although Piaget reported this category as most common among younger children, other interviewees may well be prone to it!

   Like category one (random responses), it may be a way of 'moving on' to the next question or attempting to satisfy an interviewer. With adults (or children) it may be a ploy to hide lack of knowledge or awareness of an area, or lack of previous reflection or thought, i.e. a form of bluffing or 'talking around' (circumlocution).

These five categories are derived from Piaget's work in interviewing children but they can be extended more widely. Examples of random responses, suggested conceptions, spontaneous conceptions, liberated conceptions and romancing can all be found in interview transcripts from educational research. Detecting instances of these categories of response is part of the activity of analysing interview data; the next task is to *interpret* these types of response and to reflect on what they indicate about the interviewee.

PRACTICAL APPROACHES TO ANALYSING DATA

There are all sorts of practical questions when it comes to the nitty-gritty of analysing qualitative data: Do we use a highlighting pen to seek and mark key words or should we use a computer? Should we photocopy our interview transcripts, cut them up into units then paste them together into themes/categories ... or can a computer package do this for us?

This section introduces some of the practicalities but for a full account, Riley (1990) gives a very personal, blow-by-blow, guide to dealing with data down to the level of labelling tapes, highlighting text, brainstorming and annotating records.

Returning to Research Questions

One valuable tactic when faced with a large volume of data is to return to the original research questions which were used to guide and plan the research. When data has been divided up into manageable units (either by scissors on a photocopy or on a disk) each 'unit' can be matched to a research question. By matching units to questions, piece by piece, the data gradually shed light on or illuminate those questions.

This matching of items of data to individual questions can also provide a structure for writing up and presenting research.

Looking at Language

Qualitative data most commonly consists of words, e.g. interview transcripts, documents. One strategy for analysing it is to examine the language itself (discussed more fully in Chapter 8). This can involve

1. looking for buzzwords, e.g. words which 'crept into' the language of teachers in the 1990s such as 'entitlement' or 'differentiation';
2. looking for other commonly used words and phrases by, say, an informant or an interviewee, or in documents;
3. searching for and examining commonly used metaphors. For example, teachers and lecturers now commonly use the word 'delivering' in discussing teaching and learning provision. Other common examples are 'level playing field' (in discussing competitors) and 'shifting the goalposts' (in discussing managers and

policy-makers). Such metaphors have become so embedded in the language of education that they are now 'metaphors we live by' (Lakoff and Johnson, 1980).

What do these metaphors reveal about the interviewee or document writer, e.g. their models of teaching and learning? Why have they become so commonplace? How did the 'buzzwords' in an interview transcript or a school prospectus infiltrate into our language? Where did they originate from? Are the interviewees even aware that they are using them or why?

Considering these questions is all part of the data analysis process – it may even suggest a return for more data, in order to ask informants to reflect on the language they have used (i.e. meta-data, to coin a phrase).

The guidelines and hints given here fall well short of a full content analysis of language and its use (see Krippendorf, 1980). Nor do they do justice to the importance of searching for meanings and metaphors in qualitative data. A more detailed account is given in Coffey and Atkinson (1996, ch. 4). Silverman (1993) also concentrates on the study of language in qualitative research by discussing the analysis of interviews, texts and transcripts.

Searching for Patterns and Themes
This has already been discussed in the section on stages in analysing data. The method of 'constant comparison and contrast' is well documented in the literature on research methods and, in my experience, is largely very practical and effective. As Delamont (1992) reminds people in educational research, we should search for irregularities, paradoxes and contrasts as much as patterns, themes and regularities.

One of the practical difficulties is to develop themes or categories which (a) are as mutually exclusive as possible, i.e. not too 'fuzzy' and overlapping, and (b) encompass as much data as possible without leaving too much in the inevitable 'sweeper' category of Unclassified or Miscellaneous (which, in practice, often ends up in the waste bin). This effort requires a certain amount of creativity which we look at very shortly.

Manual or Computer Labour?
Data can be sorted and analysed manually, e.g. by physically cutting up materials, doing a 'scissors-and-paste' job, sorting material into

files and folders. But computers can now be increasingly used, with appropriate software, to analyse, sort and code data.

Indeed, one of the interesting debates over the analysis of qualitative data is over whether it should be done manually or by using a suitable computer program, e.g. *Ethnograph, Textbase Alpha, Nudist* (see Tesch, 1990 for an account of most available systems; or Fielding and Lee, 1991). Tesch points out that by 'qualitative data' we often mean textual data. Indeed, textual data often means simply transcripts from interviews, text from documents or notes from observations. Some people prefer to analyse this 'manually', often by taking a copy of the text, e.g. a transcript, going through it and segmenting it (chopping it up), coding it, and perhaps categorizing it into themes, issues etc. The main human input is to discover patterns in the data by 'constant comparison' (Glaser and Strauss, 1967) or to search for 'contrasts and paradoxes' (Delamont, 1992). Computer programs can help in the process, as Tesch (1990) explains, but cannot replace the researcher's own analysis, intuition and 'craftsmanship'.

CREATIVITY IN MAKING SENSE OF QUALITATIVE DATA

Data analysis requires a person to be painstaking, thorough, systematic and meticulous. It also requires a researcher to be 'true to the data' and to make a faithful representation of the data collected, especially when presenting it and publishing it. Data collection and presentation also requires the researcher to be fair to the people involved, in giving them a platform or a voice.

On the other hand, data analysis can be enriched by an element of lateral or creative thinking. Equally, presentation involves, to some extent, providing a narrative or 'telling a story', without fabricating it. In short, creativity can play a part.

One of the best discussions I have read on this appears in Sanger *et al.* (1997, ch. 9) and the points below are an attempt to summarize some of that discussion, but with my own interpretation. Sanger actually puts forward seven 'types' of creativity in data analysis but here I focus mainly on three:

1. Using new and creative labels for categories – he describes these as labels which contain 'novel metaphoric characteristics'. As examples, he quotes metaphoric labels from the past such as: 'sink school', 'magnet' or 'beacon school', 'thick description', 'illuminative evaluation' and many others. Sanger suggests that we can

often appropriate the labels, phrases or metaphors which those being interviewed or observed use themselves.

A colleague of mine (Lorna Unwin) and I once did this by using a short sentence spoken by an apprentice in describing the Modern Apprenticeship scheme and who it is best suited to: 'It's not for the boffin'. We used this both in looking at the data and as a heading in the final report for the DfEE.

2. Using alien structures – Sanger (1997) suggests using outside, unfamiliar structures and attempting to fit the data into them. These could be adopted from other fields of inquiry but they could simply be crude frameworks forced onto the data to 'make the researcher think in new ways'. For example, attempting to impose an A–Z framework on the data. Sanger describes how forcing himself to try to identify 26 categories of issue (from A–Z) forced him to think creatively upon the data from one project. He also recounts another action research project in which a teacher analysed classroom interactions in terms of the three primary colours and mixtures of them which produced different tones.

3. Looking for metaphors in the data – this has already been discussed, but Sanger talks of it as a form of content analysis. He gives an example of classroom observation where (instead of recording verbal interactions amongst pupils) he switched his attention to examining the *metaphoric content* of pupils' talk and the images being conveyed.

Sanger's other suggested types of creativity are: using novel methods; employing 'methodological imports', i.e. approaches from totally different fields such as homeopathy or photography; using theoretical imports, i.e. attempting to employ theories or models from other areas; and writing up research in new ways (given that writing is itself a form of analysis and thinking).

Sanger's discussion is itself novel and creative – and well worth delving into further (see Sanger, 1997, especially ch. 9). My main point here is that data analysis can and should involve lateral thinking and creativity, yet still be faithful to the data and the people who provided it.

IN SUMMARY

Renata Tesch (1990) conducted her own qualitative analysis of a wide range of texts which describe and discuss the principles and procedures for analysing qualitative data. She came up with ten principles and practices which 'hold true' in qualitative analysis (in addition to the fundamental principles of honesty and correct ethical conduct in research of this kind). A summary of these principles is given below:

1. **Analysis is not the last phase in the research process; it is concurrent with data collection or cyclic**; it begins as soon as the first set of data is gathered and does not only run parallel to data collection, but the two become 'integrated' (Glaser and Strauss, 1967, p. 109). They inform or even 'drive' each other (Miles and Huberman, 1984, p. 63).
2. **The analysis process is systematic and comprehensive, but not rigid**; it proceeds in an orderly fashion and requires discipline, an organized mind and perseverance. The analysis ends only after new data no longer generate new insights; the process 'exhausts' the data.
3. **Attending to data includes a reflective activity that results in a set of analytical notes that guide the process.** 'Memos', as these analytical notes are often called, not only 'help the analyst move easily from data to conceptual level' (Miles and Huberman, 1984, p. 71), but they record the reflective and the concrete process and, therefore, provide accountability.
4. **Data are 'segmented', i.e. divided into relevant and meaningful 'units'**; yet the connection to the whole is maintained. Since the human mind is not able to process large amounts of diverse content all at once, the analyst concentrates on sets of smaller and more homogeneous chunks of material at any one time. However, the analysis always begins with reading all data to achieve 'a sense of the whole'. This sense fertilizes the interpretation of individual data pieces.
5. **The data segments are categorised according to an organizing system that is predominantly derived from the data themselves.** Large amounts of data cannot be processed unless all material that belongs together topically is assembled conceptually and physically in one place. Some topical categories, relating to a conceptual framework or to particular research questions, may exist before analysis begins, but for the most part the data are 'interrogated' with regard to the content items or themes they contain, and categories are formed as a result. The process is inductive.
6. **The main intellectual tool is comparison.** The method of comparing and contrasting is used for practically all intellectual tasks during analysis: forming categories, establishing the

boundaries of the categories, assigning data segments to categories, summarizing the content of each category, finding negative evidence etc. The goal is to discern conceptual similarities, to refine the discriminative power of categories and to discover patterns.

7. **Categories for sorting segments are tentative and preliminary in the beginning; they remain flexible**. Since categories are developed mostly from the data material during the course of analysis, they must accommodate later data. They are modified accordingly and are refined until a satisfactory system is established. Even then the categories remain flexible working tools, not rigid end products.

8. **Manipulating qualitative data during analysis is an eclectic activity; there is no one 'right' way**. The researchers who have described the procedures they have used to analyse text data usually are wary about 'prescriptions'. They wish to avoid standardizing the process, since one hallmark of qualitative research is the creative involvement of the individual researcher. There is no fixed formula: 'It is possible to analyse any phenomenon in more than one way' (Spradley, 1979, p. 92).

9. **The procedures are neither 'scientific' nor 'mechanistic'**; qualitative analysis is 'intellectual craftsmanship'. On the one hand, there are no strict rules that can be followed mindlessly; on the other hand, the researcher is not allowed to be limitlessly inventive. Qualitative analysis can and should be done 'artfully' even 'playfully' (Goetz and Le Compte, 1984, p. 172), but it also requires a great amount of methodological knowledge and intellectual competence.

10. **The result of the analysis is some type of higher-level synthesis**. While much work in the analysis process consists of 'taking apart' (for instance, into smaller pieces), the final goal is the emergence of a larger, consolidated picture.

(adapted from Tesch, 1990, pp. 95–7)

Her claim is that if 'a researcher adheres to these principles and commits no logical or ethical errors, her/his work will qualify as scholarly qualitative data analysis' (*Ibid.*, 1990, p. 97).

Writing

> That we would do,
> We should do when we would
> (*Hamlet*, Act 4, Scene 7)

In urging himself not to procrastinate, Shakespeare's Prince of Denmark was talking of revenge for his father's death rather than writing his article, thesis or book. But the same general rules might apply: start writing from day one, and remember the rhyme: 'Don't get it right, get it written.'

This chapter is about the writing process. It consists of a mixture of handy hints, rules of thumb and guidelines, and some basic, but important, points about punctuation and proofreading.

Really good research writing is much harder to pin down and define, however. Woods (1999) provides an excellent discussion of what he calls successful writing. One of his criteria for good writing is what he calls 'attention to detail'. He quotes the novelist David Lodge who describes how he learnt to 'use a few selected details, heightened by metaphor and simile, to evoke character or the sense of place' (quoted in *Ibid.*, p. 13). This art, or craft, applies equally well to writing on education. Woods also talks of the importance of being able to express these in writing. The ability to connect or synthesize ideas is actually an aspect of creativity which sometimes shows itself in educational writing and research. It might be the ability to connect and interrelate one's own findings with existing research or theory, it might be a synthesis of ideas from two completely different domains of knowledge, e.g. using literature from a seemingly unrelated area, or it might be the application of a theory or model from one field to a totally new area. Synthesis or connections of this kind can be risky, and require a degree of self-confidence, but they can be illuminating.

In discussing the writing up of qualitative research, Woods (1999, pp. 54–6) also talks of the importance of including 'other voices' in the text, besides that of the author. One of the objectives of educational research is to give people (teachers, students, pupils, parents) a voice or a platform, and this must be reflected in the written medium by which the research is made public. Giving people a voice, however, leads to some difficult choices. Every write-up is finite. Do you include lengthy statements or transcripts from one or two people, or many shorter points from a larger variety? (See Woods, 1999, p. 56 for discussion.)

A final point made by Woods concerns the importance, when writing, of not missing the humorous side of research, e.g. by including an ironic comment from an interviewee.

There are many features which together make up 'good' research writing – and they are much easier to recognize than to define. Two excellent sources are the Woods' book, already cited, and H. S. Becker's 1986 classic which we return to near the end of the chapter.

A LINGUISTIC CHALLENGE

Educational research has been criticized for its inaccessibility. Sometimes this criticism is unfounded because educational research needs to be challenging and thought-provoking. However, there are times when the attempt to be profound, creative and original leads almost to self-parody. I recently attended a conference on the history and philosophy of science in education where the following abstract appeared in the handbook. It is reproduced anonymously here exactly as it was printed:

> *Knowledge Agendas: From Metaphors of Nature to Metaphors of Culture*
> This paper offers a reading of the call for grounding of the runaway concept generation released by the weakening of Galilean paradigm. It seeks this grounding in terms of a link between the epistemological issues underlying the shift from Kantian objects of yesterday to quasi-objects of tomorrow and the possibility of developing empirical relations between competing parametrizations of knowledge domains. It aims at rescuing experimentation and technology from the status of actualization of metaphysics and at restoring their originary role in constituting and re-constituting the material reality into recognizable units. Finally, it outlines briefly a research program aimed at pursuing this line of enquiry in institutions of education and learning.

I spent an entire term as an undergraduate studying Immanuel Kant's work but this paragraph still defeats me.

Even books on education and educational research which are generally well written and thought-provoking can provide the occasional sentence which puzzles the linguistically challenged such as myself. In an excellent book on educational research the following sentence occurs in a section discussing 'post-colonialism':

> By failing 'properly' to return the objectivizing gaze of the colonizer, to provide the fully delineated, and perversely desired, Other that would secure the Self of the colonizer, the fractured identity of the subaltern profoundly destabilizes, in turn, the Western idea (ideal) of the universal human subject. (Stronach and Maclure, 1996, p. 59)

I am still struggling with this sentence.

There is a danger, particularly for new writers who are striving to display their initiation into academic discourse, of 'shooting from the hip' with newly acquired buzzwords. Jargon can be valuable; terms such as 'ontology', 'epistemology', 'paradigm', 'qualitative', 'triangulation', 'validity', and so on (see Glossary) all refer to important concepts, but they can easily be strung together to form a grammatical but totally meaningless sentence:

> The elusive epistemology of Smith's ambiguous ontology results in a problematic contestation of the discourse of reflexive dialectic, hybridizing the hermeneutic parameters of discursive dialogue and transgressing the shifting boundaries of hegemonic signifiers.

WRITING FOR DIFFERENT AUDIENCES

The main purpose of writing up educational research is to communicate with other people (although this is not always obvious when reading it). It is hardly worth doing research if it is not disseminated. Communication can, and should, take place with a number of different audiences in mind: one's peers and fellow-researchers, practitioners, policy-makers, curriculum planners and developers, teachers or lecturers, parents or the general public. Once again the ground rule is horses for courses: 'Different purposes and different audiences require different styles of writing' (Woods, 1999, p. 48). In addition, different aims and audiences require different

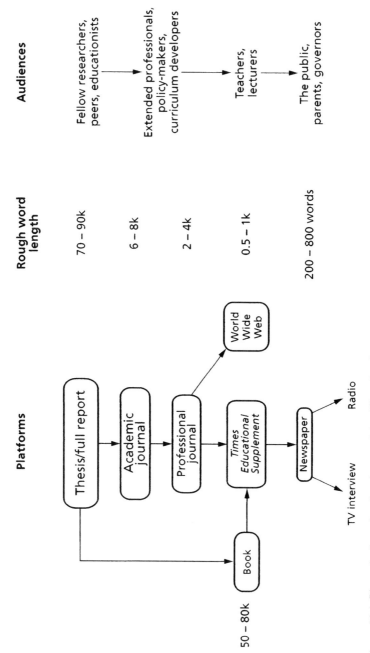

Figure 11.1: Disseminating educational research for different audiences

lengths of writing. Figure 11.1 shows possible examples of different 'platforms' for writing, of different length for different audiences.

An interesting author on 'writing for diverse audiences' is Richardson (1985, 1987 and 1990). From a piece of research on single women in relationships with married men, she published both academic journal articles and a populist book (*The New Other Woman*). Peter Woods (1999, pp. 48–50) discusses the way she varied her language, her style, her tone and the structure in her writing for different audiences. Woods himself gives an example of writing for different audiences from his own research into 'critical events' in schools. This was disseminated via an academic journal article focusing on the theory emerging from the research; another journal article concentrating on the pupils' perspectives, including case study material; and a reader for students training to be primary teachers with a catchy title including the term 'exceptional educational events'. The latter included only eight references, the former contained over a hundred.

One of my own experiences relating to Figure 11.1 has been to convert my PhD thesis into a book (Wellington, 1989, on the links between education and employment). The book (about 60,000 words long) was considerably shorter than the thesis (about 100,000 words including all the appendices). The book omitted large chunks of qualitative data and most of the discussion on methodology which appeared in the thesis.

Book proposals require considerable thought, partly because, unlike theses, books have to be sold, meaning that somebody must want to buy them. My experience with publishers and their commissioning editors is that they are extremely helpful and will support a good idea, even if it will not result in tens of thousands of books sold. The editor who commissioned the book you are now reading offered the valuable guidelines to writing book proposals shown in Box 11.1.

TO STRUCTURE, OR NOT TO STRUCTURE

There is considerable debate about how much structure authors should include in writing up a report, thesis, book or article. This section considers structure at three levels: overall contents structure; within chapters; and at sentence level.

Headings, Sub-headings, Sub-sub-headings . . .
Headings are valuable signposts in guiding a reader through a text and maintaining interest or concentration. But it is always difficult to

Box 11.1: How to submit a perfect book proposal

I've been asked several times what I want to see in a book proposal. Below is a pretty exhaustive guide. Not every point in it will apply to every proposal. Three sides of A4 is usually sufficient, four sides is usually ample.

1. Summarize the book in a few lines at the start, including a working title.
2. Outline the contents. It is often useful to do this chapter by chapter.
3. Say how long the book will be, to the nearest 5,000 words, and how many illustrations, tables etc. it will include.
4. Identify the intended market(s).
   (a) Avoid Uncle Tom Cobleigh sentences ('This book is intended for classroom teachers, middle management, senior management, ITT students and their tutors and mentors, researchers, lecturers, advisers, administrators, policy-makers . . .). It may well be that your book would appeal to more than one of these groups, but it would be helpful to distinguish between main and subsidiary audiences.
   (b) Quantify the market as far as possible. For example, if your book is aimed at a certain type of course, how many such courses are there? And how many students are there on such courses?
   (c) Identify courses for which your book might make recommended or essential reading.
   (d) Explain how your book would appeal, e.g. through contributors, references, case studies, to different national markets, e.g. Scotland, Ireland, the EU, North America, Australia.
5. Analyse the competition:
   (a) What comparable books are there? How does your book compare/contrast?
   (b) If there isn't a comparable book, suggest why there isn't.
6. Present yourself as author/editor.
   (a) Give your title, affiliation and relevant qualification.
   (b) Give a brief bibliography of your relevant publications, annotated to identify the kind of audience if this is less than obvious.
   (c) Mention any relevant networks you belong to (e.g. conferences you attend, associations to which you belong).
   (d) Explain your affective involvement: why does this matter to you? What is at stake for you?
7. By when could you submit the manuscript? Avoid good intentions here – be realistic.
8. What's in it for the reader? Finally, it is useful to summarize the benefits the book offers to the reader. Many of these will be implicit in much of the above, but it is worth spelling out what's in it for the reader.
9. Include contact numbers, including fax and e-mail where available.

Source: Anthony Haynes, Commissioning Editor for Education, Continuum

decide how many levels of headings to use. Some 'headings' are essential, even if it is just the title of a book or report. Below that, most people would agree that chapter headings are essential. But how far 'down' do we go in imposing structure on our writing?

The example in Box 11.2 show two possible lists of contents for an archaeology thesis.

Box 11.2: Degrees of structure: two possible lists of contents

The first simply uses chapter headings. The second uses sub-headings (e.g. 1.1), sub-sub-headings (e.g. 1.1.3), sub-sub-sub-headings (e.g. 1.1.3.4) and sub-sub-sub-sub-headings (e.g. 2.1.1.3.2). The author has clearly attempted to plan this thesis in the finest detail and may well be able to follow these levels right down to the dungeons of logic. But can the reader cope with a structure of this kind? My view is that they cannot. Once we get past the 'sub-sub' level we begin to flounder. For me, this is the lowest level to use.

Book editors always advise authors to be clear, when writing, about the level of heading they are using at any given time. Headings are then given a level (in my case level A, level B and level C) and each level uses a different font or typeface.

For example:
Level A: **CHAPTER HEADINGS** (upper case, bold)
Level B: **Sub-headings** (lower case, bold)
Level C: *Sub-sub-headings* (lower case, italics)

Writers then need to be (or at least try to be) clear and consistent about which headings they are using and why. If a writer goes 'below' level C this can be difficult.

Chapter Structure

Headings and sub-headings can help to structure a chapter and break it down into digestible chunks. But there is also a useful rule, followed by many writers, which can help to give a chapter a feeling of coherence or tightness. This rule suggests that a chapter should have three (unequal in size) parts:

- a short introduction, explaining what the author is going to write about;
- the main body, presenting the substance of the chapter; and
- a concluding section, rounding off the chapter.

This overall pattern works well for many writers, and readers, especially in a thesis or a research report. It is rather like the old adage associated with preaching: 'Tell them what you're going to say, then say it, and then tell them what you've just said.' For many types or genres of writing it works well and assists coherence. However, if overdone it can be slightly tedious.

One other way of improving coherence is to write link sentences joining one paragraph to the next or linking chapters. For example, the last sentence (or paragraph) of a chapter could be a signal or an appetizer leading into the next.

Connecting Phrases and Sentences

One of the important devices in writing is the logical connective. Connectives are simply linking words and can be used to link ideas within a sentence, to link sentences or to link one paragraph to the next. Examples include: 'First', 'Secondly', 'Thirdly', 'Finally'; also 'However', 'Nevertheless', 'Moreover', 'Interestingly', 'Furthermore', 'In addition', 'In conclusion', 'Thus', and so on.

Connectives can be valuable in maintaining a flow or a logical sequence in writing; but be warned – readers can suffer from an overdose if they are used too liberally, especially if the same one is used repeatedly. Ten 'howevers' on the same page can become wearing.

All the tactics and strategies summarized above have the same general aim: to improve clarity and communication. Table 11.1 gives a summary of four useful strategies which can be used in writing, whether it be an article, a book or a thesis.

Table 11.1: Four useful strategies in structuring writing

Strategy	Meaning	Examples
Signposting	Giving a map to the reader; outlining the structure and content of an essay, thesis or chapter, i.e. structure statements	This chapter describes . . . The first section discusses . . . This paper is structured as follows . . .
Framing	Indicating beginnings and endings of sections, topics, chapters	Firstly, . . . Finally, . . . To begin with . . . This chapter ends with . . . To conclude . . .
Linking	Joining sentence to sentence, section to section, chapter to chapter . . .	It follows that . . . The next section goes on to . . . As we saw in the last chapter . . . Therefore, . . .
Focusing	Highlighting, emphasizing, reinforcing, key points	As mentioned earlier . . . The central issue is . . . Remember that . . . It must be stressed that . . .

THINGS WHICH THE SPELLCHECKER MISSES

Spellcheckers are marvellous things but they are no substitute for human proofreaders.

> OWED TO SPELL CHECKERS
> I have a spelling checker
> I disk covered four my PC.
> It plane lee marks four my revue
> Miss steaks aye can knot see.
>
> Eye ran this poem threw it.
> Your sure real glad two no.
> Its very polished in its weigh,
> My checker tolled me sew.
>   (original source unknown)

In my experience of writing and reading, the four most common areas where vigilant proofreading is needed are

1. Missing apostrophes, e.g. 'The pupils book was a complete mess. Its true to say that apostrophes are a problem.'
2. Unwanted apostrophes, e.g. 'The pupil's made a complete mess. It's bone was a source of amusement.' (The use of 'it's' for 'its', and vice versa, is a common mistake.)
3. Referencing: referring to items in the text which are not listed in the list of references at the end, and vice versa, i.e. listing references which are not included in the text.
4. Commonly misused words: effect/affect; criterion/criteria; phenomenon/phenomena; their/there.

Further guidelines, which are offered as a checklist when writing, are given in Appendices 2 and 3.

WRITING UP: A FEW PARTING THOUGHTS

For the sake of brevity here, a list of twelve suggestions and guidelines on writing is given below, as concisely as possible (for further discussion, an excellent source is Becker, 1986).

1. Treat writing as a 'form of thinking' (Becker, 1986). Writing does not proceed by having preset thoughts which are then transformed onto paper. Instead, thoughts are created and developed by the process of writing. Writing up your work is an excellent, albeit slightly painful, way of thinking through and making sense of what you have done or what you're doing. This is a good reason for not leaving writing until the end; writing should begin immediately.
2. Expose it to a friend – find a reader/colleague whom you can trust to be reliable and just, but critical. Look for somebody else, perhaps someone with no expertise in the area, to read your writing and comment on it. They, and you, should ask: Is it clear? Is it readable? Is it well-structured, e.g. do you need more subheadings? In other words use other people, use books, e.g. style manuals, books on writing. And don't do your own proofreading.
3. Draft and redraft; write and rewrite – and don't either expect or try to get it right first time. Writing up, especially if you have a word processor, should not be treated as a 'once and for all' activity. Getting the first draft on to paper is just the first stage.
4. Remove unnecessary words; make each word work for a living. After the first draft is on paper go back and check for excess baggage, i.e. redundant words and circumlocution.

5. Avoid tired/hackneyed metaphors like 'cutting edge' and 'huge terrain', and overdone sayings like 'falling between two stools' and 'the bottom line'.

6. Think carefully about when you should use an *active* voice in your sentences and when a *passive* voice may or may not help. The passive voice can be a useful way of depersonalizing sentences but sometimes naming the 'active agent' helps clarity and gives more information, e.g. 'Jane Smith, the IT co-ordinator, bought three new computers' (active voice), compared with 'Three new computers were bought' (passive). Giles and Hedge (1994) give fuller discussion of this point (p. 89) and many other aspects of writing (chs 4, 5).

7. Feel free to admit, in writing, that you found it hard to decide on the 'right way' to, for example, organize your material, decide on a structure, get started, write the conclusion, etc. Don't be afraid to say this in the text.

8. Vary sentence length; use a few really short ones now and again, e.g. four words. These can have a real impact.

9. Edit 'by ear'; make sure it sounds right and feels right. Treat writing as somewhat like talking to someone except that now you are communicating with the written word. Keep your readers in mind at all times, better still, one *particular* reader. What will they make of this sentence? It can help if you visualize your reader(s) as you are writing.

   But, unlike talking, the reader only has what is on paper. Readers, unlike listeners, do not have body language, tone of voice or any knowledge of you, your background or your thoughts. Writers cannot make the assumptions and short cuts that can be made between talkers and listeners.

10. Readers need guidance, especially to a large thesis or book. In the early pages, brief the readers on what they are about to receive. Provide a map to help them navigate through it.

11. Break a large piece of writing down into manageable chunks or pieces which will gradually fit together. I call this the 'jigsaw puzzle' approach – but an overall plan is still needed to fit all the pieces together. The pieces will also require linking together. The job of writing link sentences and link paragraphs joining section to section and chapter to chapter, is vital for coherence and fluency.

12. Above all, get it 'out of the door' (Becker, 1986) for your friendly reader to look at. Don't sit on it for months, 'polishing' it. Get it

off your desk, give it to someone to read, then work on it again
when it comes back.

Finally, two of the common problems in writing are (a) getting
started (b) writing the abstract and introduction. You can avoid the
first by not trying to find the 'one right way' first time round (Becker,
1986), and the second by leaving the introduction and abstract until
last. Writing with a word processor helps to ease both.

WORKING TOWARDS A THESIS

For people doing research towards a thesis, here are a few extra 'tips'
which might be helpful:

1. Read some past theses at this level which are in your area.
2. As you are writing, keep full bibliographical details (including
   page numbers) of everything you refer to. *Not* doing this is one of
   my own favourite failings and leads to a lot of annoying and time-
   consuming work at the end.
3. Keep a *Research Diary*: this should hold a record of your reading,
   your fieldwork, your thinking and your planning.
4. Ask someone to comment on your plan and your writing style at
   any early stage.
5. Set yourself short-term targets (e.g. sections of a chapter) and a
   timetable and try to keep to them. If you can't, or don't, ask
   yourself why.
6. Talk to people other than your supervisor about your thesis, e.g.
   friends, colleagues.

As for the structure and format of the final report, thesis or
dissertation there is considerable debate. On one hand, some argue
that a wide range of formats and styles is acceptable, i.e. there is no
standard format for a report or thesis; on the other, some favour a rigid,
'logical' structure, following the traditional sequence of Introduction,
Literature Review, Methods, Results, Conclusion, Bibliography,
Appendices. Table 11.2 gives a summary of the traditional structure
for a thesis.

A counter-argument to this view is that a neat, 'logical' format for a
thesis misrepresents the messy nature of real research (first argued by
Medawar, 1963). My own view is that a writer has a certain
obligation to convey to readers *how* the research was done, *what* was
studied and *why*, the main claims put forward and the evidence for
them. This can be achieved while at the same time explaining the

Table 11.2: The traditional structure for a dissertation

Abstract	What you did Why it is important How you did it Key findings
Introduction	Main aims Key research questions Scene-setting/the context of the study A 'map' for the reader
Literature review	
Methodology and methods	Which methods Why these The sample
Results/findings/analysis	
Discussion and evaluation	Reflection on both findings and methods Relation to existing literature
Conclusions and recommendations	Contributions and limitations So what . . .? What are the implications of your work? Ideas for further research
Appendices	E.g. interview schedule Detailed tables of data
References/bibliography	

messy, disorderly nature of the actual research process within the report or thesis. My own view thus agrees with Hammersley (1995, p. 96) who argues that

> all research texts must be seen as presenting an argument, and in doing so must make explicit certain essential components. These consist of five sorts of information that readers need access to: about the focus of the study, about the case(s) investigated, about the methods employed, about the main claims made and the evidence offered in support of them, and about the conclusions drawn.

Box 11.3: What makes a good thesis?

The 'best' theses

- consider a wide range of literature (including at least one or two references which make the reader say 'Ah! That's a new one.');
- are well-structured and clear to follow;
- embed their own work in the work of others;
- deliberate on methods and methodology *before* their own empirical work;
- are honest and open about the methods they have used, and why;
- reflect back on their methods and methodology *after* they have reported their work;
- contain few typos, clumsy sentences or incorrect use of words (e.g., 'effect' for 'affect', 'it's' for 'its', 'criterion' for 'criteria');
- generalize from their own work, or at least make explicit the lessons which can be learnt from it; but also
- bring out their own limitations (without being apologetic) and suggest areas for further research;
- pull out practical implications for policy-makers or practitioners or both;
- contribute to the 'public store of knowledge' – even, perhaps, the 'public good' – not just the writer's own personal development.

−12

What's the use of educational research?

SUSTAINED ATTACK ... BUT NOTHING NEW?

You don't need to be a dedicated follower of the media to realize that educational research was the target for fairly regular, and often emotive, criticism at the end of the last century. Figure 12.1 shows a collage of some fairly typical newspaper headlines in 1997, 1998 and 1999. Educational research was accused (with some justification) of being a 'secret' or 'walled garden', described as 'thriving though possibly tangled with weeds' (Patricia Rowan in the *TES*, 19.3.99, p. 15).

One regular critic of educational research (Alan Smithers, then of Manchester University) who frequently poured vitriol on most research (except his own) demanded that 'social usefulness' should be the gauge by which educational research is measured. Again, he had a point, but his sometimes perceptive criticisms were often seen as ammunition coming from the same gun as a rather less tactful

Figure 12.1: Educational research in the media spotlight

opponent, the Chief Inspector of Schools, Chris Woodhead. Woodhead, or 'woodentop', as some of his detractors nicknamed him, accused educational research by academics of being biased and irrelevant 'dross' (*The Times*, 23.7.98). He singled out qualitative research which did not 'stand up to scrutiny', and described it as 'woolly and simplistic', a 'massive waste of taxpayers' money'. Woodhead's attack followed the publication of a report by James Tooley. Tooley had examined 41 articles in four educational journals and concluded that only 37 per cent of them met his criteria of 'good practice'.

In the next section we consider Tooley's critique, an important report by Hillage *et al*. (1998) and some influential analysis by David Hargreaves. But first, it needs to be noted that attacks on educational research are not a new phenomenon. The history of formal schooling for all is fairly short. Similarly, formal research into education is no more than about 100 years of age. In her summary of the history of educational research in the USA, Ellen Lagemann (1997) uses the metaphor of a 'contested terrain'. She argues that the period 1890–1990 saw a 'continuous litany of complaints' over the validity and the usefulness or value of educational research: 'one of the most notable aspects of the history of education research has been the constancy with which the enterprise has been subjected to criticism' (p. 5). On the positive side, she does cite two studies which have shown the important impact research has had on teaching and education (Clifford, 1973 and Suppes, 1978, though it is worth noting that both publications were in the 1970s). On the negative side, she points out that 'education research has not yielded dramatic improvements in practice of the kind one can point to in Medicine' (this analogy with medicine appears again shortly).

Lagemann's explanation for the 'contested terrain' is that the key questions of what education research is, who it is for and who should conduct and appraise it have continually 'pitted many groups against one another'. These groups, or professions, have vied with each other for the territory of educational research, leading to conflict and competition between 'scholars of education', teachers, administrators, professional organizations and government agencies over the content, conduct and usage of educational research. Her explanation is based on a 'system-of-professions' theory which views professionalization as 'an ongoing competition to secure jurisdiction in particular domains of human service' (Lagemann, 1997, p. 5).

Lagemann's theory for explaining the contested terrain of educational research in the USA may well be supported by recent criticisms of its condition in the UK, which we now consider briefly.

CRITICS AND CRITICISMS OF EDUCATIONAL RESEARCH IN THE LATE 1990s

Cynicism and scepticism for educational research may well have flourished among the teaching profession for several decades (the 'chalkface' viewing the 'ivory tower') but the period 1996–9 saw the publication of a new and unprecedented range of critiques of educational research from within the research profession itself. We cannot consider each one in depth here but the main areas of criticism, and the responses they provoked, are well worth summarizing.

Hargreaves
The first major landmark in this series of self-examination can, with the benefit of hindsight, be seen to be David Hargreaves' Teacher Training Agency (TTA) annual lecture in 1996. Hargreaves argued that the effectiveness of school teaching could be greatly improved if teaching were a 'research-based profession' (p. 1). Blame for the fact that it allegedly is *not*, was laid squarely on the *researchers* (a 'conflicting profession', perhaps, in Lagemann's (1997) analysis). Researchers have failed to provide an agreed, cumulative 'knowledge base' which could be used as a guide to the 'solution of practical problems' (p. 2). Unlike Medicine or the natural sciences, much educational research was 'non-cumulative' involving unconnected small-scale investigations which are not built upon or followed up. These 'inevitably produce inconclusive and contestable findings of little worth' (*Idem*). He described (probably correctly) *replications* in educational research as 'astonishingly rare', and yet highly necessary because of the importance of 'contextual and cultural variations'.

Hargreaves summarizes his own criticisms of educational research by saying:

> what would come to an end is the frankly second-rate educational research which does not make a serious contribution to fundamental theory or knowledge; which is irrelevant to practice; which is uncoordinated with any preceding or follow-up research; and which clutters up academic journals that virtually nobody reads. (p. 7)

His proposal is for a new and 'very different kind of research' which would influence practice and be based on the active involvement of 'user communities, practitioners and policy-makers' in 'all aspects of the research process' (p. 6). This would be generated by the establishment of a National Educational Research Forum which would stimulate, he hoped, 'evidence-based research relating to what teachers do in classrooms' (p. 7).

Many teachers and researchers would enthusiastically agree with Hargreaves' views as summarized thus far: educational research should be accessible, relevant to practice and cumulative; and it should involve more co-operation between different communities or professions. However, many (myself included) would take issue with two of Hargreaves' other points. The first is a kind of throwaway line when he asks:

> just how much research is there which (i) demonstrates conclusively that if teachers change their practice from x to y there will be a significant and enduring improvement in teaching and learning and (ii) has developed an effective method of convincing teachers of the benefits of, and means to, changing from x to y? (p. 8)

This belief in a kind of obvious causality, direct causal relationships, or clearly measurable and identifiable *impact* is based on an unrealistic view of research, not only in education but also in modern science.

Hargreaves' other *faux pas*, in my opinion, was to hold medicine up as a model of a research-based (or 'evidence-based' – a term used synonymously) profession. As Hammersley (1997, pp. 149–54) points out at length in his response to Hargreaves, the analogy stands up to very little analysis.

The weakness in using this analogy is that it is based on a false conception of medicine as a truly research-based profession (remember the attempts to compare educational research with an outdated, idealized model of the natural sciences). Hargreaves claims that in Medicine 'there is little difference between researchers and users: all are practitioners'; this is in contrast to education where 'researchers are rarely users' (p. 3). But the idea of medicine as a unified profession, where all are engaged in research and whose practice is based upon it, hardly stands up even to common-sense analysis. There are surely many separate and conflicting professions (Lagemann, 1997) in the field of medicine just as there are in education. The practice of some may be based on research (especially if they are engaged in it) but the practice of others (an isolated general practitioner for example) may be far less research-based.

Hargreaves also chose an unfortunate time at which to hold medicine up as a model to which education might aspire. As Hammersley (1997) points out (by citing Altman (1994)), medical research had already been found as guilty of flaws in design, conduct and methodology as had educational research:

> When I tell friends outside Medicine that many papers published in medical journals are misleading because of methodological weaknesses they are rightly shocked. Huge sums of money are spent annually on research that is seriously flawed through use of inappropriate designs, unrepresentative samples, small samples, incorrect methods of analysis, and faulty interpretation. (Altman, 1994, p. 283)

Hammersley also refers the reader to earlier work by Anderson, B., 1990.

As fate would have it, Hargreaves' 1996 article was followed, in June 1998, by several damning attacks, unconnected with his TTA lecture, on the concept of medicine as an honourable research-based profession. *The Lancet* of 13 June 1998 carried a short article headed: LIES, DAMNED LIES AND EVIDENCE-BASED MEDICINE. The author (D. P. Kernick) talked of the importance of 'learning to live with the uncertainty of most of the grey zones in Medicine'. Kernick talked very sensibly of decisions being based on a 'cognitive continuum'. The article, worth reading in full, puts paid to Hargreaves' simplistic hope of research proving that X is more effective than Y.

The medical profession was further analysed by newspaper articles with headings such as: HOW DOCTORS HAVE BETRAYED US ALL (*The Independent on Sunday*, 14 June 1998). The medical establishment was described as 'arrogant, secretive and unaccountable'.

And finally, the exposure was given a wider airing by a Channel 4 programme in the same week called 'The Citadel', which took a similar line.

Perhaps this all goes to show the danger of holding something or someone up as a model. Such an exercise, like pride, inevitably comes before a fall, rather like several politicians in the same era who pontificated on morality and family values shortly before being exposed with their 'trousers down'.

However, Hargreaves' (1996) critique of educational research did contain several important points, despite the unfortunate suggestion that research can establish clear causal links and the mis-timed comparison with medicine as a role model. In a later, less polemical, article (Hargreaves, 1999) he reiterated his important criticisms and admitted that it might be best to talk of 'evidence-*informed*' policy and practice rather than evidence-*based*. But by then, unfortunately, damage had been done. Some of the cruder points of his first critique had crept into the language and rhetoric of the Teacher Training Agency (Cordingley, 1999) and the simplistic model of crude causal connections had even permeated the thinking of the Economic and Social Research Council (ESRC). Their Chief Executive, Professor Amman announced a new £12 million programme of educational research with the words: 'This new programme will be seeking to develop evidence-based teaching showing what works best and why it does so' (cited in Hargreaves, 1999, p. 245, but clearly based on Hargreaves' earlier critique). Hargreaves' (1999, p. 247) more carefully considered article, in 1999, spoke of:

1. the role of evidence/research as being to 'inform, not determine, policy and practice';
2. a recognition that 'scientific conclusiveness' is a 'matter of degree';
3. and an 'understanding that discovering "what works" is not a search for universal laws but an uncovering of ever-changing practices through a research process that is itself endless'.

Tooley, Darby and Ofsted (1997–8)
An article which was just as damaging and widely publicized as Hargreaves' 1996 critique, and equally provocative, was published by Ofsted in 1998. The Chief Inspector of Schools, Chris Woodhead, had, in a public lecture in 1997 declared that educational research made 'blindingly obvious statements' in 'impenetrable' language that was 'hostile' to the Conservative government of the time and to 'any future Labour government' (Woodhead, 1997, pp. 3–4). He therefore commissioned an inquiry into educational research to be led by James Tooley, then of Manchester University. The resultant inquiry focused on a purposive sample of 41 articles taken from four education journals. Unsurprisingly, Tooley found that 63 per cent of them did not match his criteria of 'good practice'. The report identified several 'themes' in its survey of the 41 articles which included:

1. partisanship - in the conduct of the research, its presentation and its arguments (only a small minority of articles showed a 'detached, non-partisan approach');
2. methodological problems, e.g. lack of triangulation, bias in sampling; and

3. poor presentation, e.g. lack of reporting of sample size and method of sample selection: 'It was indicative of the cavalier approach of many researchers that even simple factual details such as the sample size and how it was selected were often considered to be irrelevant to the reader' (Tooley and Darby, 1998, p. 46)
4. the focus of the research: the relevance of some articles to policy and practice was said to be 'tenuous at best'; there were no examples of replication of earlier work; and a picture 'emerged of researchers doing their research largely in a vacuum, un-noticed and unheeded by anyone else'. (p. 6)

The 82-page report received extensive press coverage and whole-hearted support from its initiator, Chris Woodhead. Many of the points made, of course, were linked with the earlier article by Hargreaves (1996). In retaliation, the critics of 'Tooley and Darby' (and there was no shortage), accused the report of being itself partisan and methodologically flawed.

The Hillage Report (1998)
A more widely respected report followed closely on Tooley and Woodhead's heels. The Department for Education and Employment commissioned the Institute for Employment Studies to review the state of educational research *relating to schools in England*. Evidence was collected by a literature review, interviews with 40 key 'stake-holders', a 'call for evidence' from various interested groups and a further set of focus groups, and interviews with teachers, advisers and inspectors.

The outcome was a detailed report, written in carefully measured tones, on the state of 'research on schools'. The report, over 80 pages long, deserves to be read in full. For brevity here, we summarize its main *criticisms* of ER as tending to be

1. often too 'small-scale' to be reliable and generalizable;
2. not based on existing knowledge;
3. presented in an inaccessible form or medium; and
4. not interpreted for an audience of practitioners or policy-makers.

These criticisms echo remarkably the earlier critiques of Hargreaves (1996) and, to some extent, the less measured attacks by Woodhead and the Tooley report of 1998. They may not all be singing from the same 'hymn-sheet' but the criticisms can fairly easily be combined together and summarized. This has been done in the form of ten points (see Box 12.1).

Box 12.1: A cumulation of recent criticisms of educational research

1. **irrelevant** to practitioners and policy-makers;
2. **non-cumulative**, i.e. not co-ordinated to previous or follow-up research; not based on an existing body of knowledge ... or contributing to it;
3. **inaccessible**, exclusive;
4. **unreadable**, impenetrable, poorly written;
5. **supply** (i.e. researcher) driven rather than **demand** (i.e. user-group) driven;
6. not **interpreted** for a practitioner or policy-making audience;
7. no **impact** on policy or practice;
8. biased, **partisan**;
9. tending towards '**political correctness**';
10. **small-scale**, unreliable, not generalizable.

Source: Based on Hargreaves (1996), Woodhead (1997), Hillage *et al.* (1998) and Tooley and Darby (1998)

Box 12.1 gives a summary of the criticisms of educational research that accumulated over a remarkably brief period (1996–8) in its short history. Many of these criticisms are well founded. Others, as discussed already, are based on mistaken conceptions of what educational research, or indeed any research, could achieve – or on unhelpful analogies with other areas which are at least as susceptible to criticism.

The main value of this short era of criticism has been in forcing educational research to look not only at itself but also at its connection with others, i.e. policy-makers and practitioners. This area, of connection and collaboration, is the area we look at next.

EDUCATIONAL RESEARCH, POLICY AND PRACTICE

Several valuable ideas emerged from Hargreaves (1996, 1999), the Hillage report (1998) and other discussions of educational research in the same era. The idea of a 'national education research framework' was mooted in Hillage. The establishment of a National Education Research Forum was suggested both by Hargreaves and by the Hillage report – the first such body was created at the end of 1999. Hillage *et al.* also suggested 'policy fora' which would link researchers, policy-makers and practitioners.

One of the key ideas which emerged was that of 'user-groups' for educational research – an idea which was given teeth by making links to user groups one of the criteria for assessing universities on their research rating. This became included as part of the Research Assessment Exercise. The impact of research on practice (and policy) is now part of the assessment process. Consequently, the term 'user-group' has become embedded in the discourse.

But just who or what are these user groups? What 'use' might they make of Research? How might 'users' be involved in research? And how can research be communicated to users and user groups?

One obviously flawed model is the conveyor belt or coffee-machine model shown in the cartoon in Figure 12.2. In this model, research is 'done', written up, stored and made available to 'users' like a commodity. Practitioners or policy-makers can avail themselves of it as and when they require a quick dose, rather like the teacher in the cartoon.

This metaphor, of one group providing a 'commodity' to another (who may take it or leave it), is clearly unacceptable as a future model. The model, which Hillage *et al.* and others were anxious to set up, is of an interaction between practitioners, policy-makers and researchers at all stages of the research process. As Hillage *et al.* pointed out (1998, p. xi), research effort should not be 'predominantly

Figure 12.2: Requiring a quick dose
Source: Drawing by David Houchin

Table 12.1: User groups in educational research

1. Categories of 'user'
- planners/builders of education 'spaces', e.g. rooms, labs, schools
- teachers, lecturers
- policy-makers
- employers
- unions
- community groups
- other researchers
- curriculum developers/planners
- advisers, inspectors
- parents
- campaign groups, charities
- subject organizations, e.g. Association for Science Education (ASE)
- textbook writers, software producers

2. Possible uses these groups might make of research
- to inform teaching
- in campaigning, advocating
- to improve practice or policy
- to guide policy
- to improve awareness or knowledge, e.g. by employers
- to develop/improve curricula
- to inform their own research

3. Possible user involvement in the research process
- as participants or collaborators (e.g. teacher-researchers)
- as key informants
- as the 'objects' of research, e.g. employers, teachers
- as initiators of research or co-researchers

4. Possible means of communicating with 'users'
- magazines, newspapers, education supplements
- talks at conferences
- the Web/Internet
- publications, e.g. books, journals
- pamphlets
- teaching programmes, e.g. diploma, masters
- subject and other associations
- newsletters
- courses for teachers (INSET)
- radio/television
- exchanges, visits, secondments

supply (i.e. researcher) driven'. A dialogue is needed between researchers and users.

Table 12.1 is an attempt to summarize the main groups who might be involved in this dialogue and *how* they might be involved.

The Impact of Research on Policy and Practice
Table 12.1 offers a very simplistic view and much remains to be said on the dialogue between researchers and 'users', and the very concept of user groups. Indeed, the whole area of the impact of research on policy and practice is itself the subject of extensive research and publication. This section summarizes some of the issues and explanations in that area.

One valuable observation was made by my colleague Peter Hannon. He describes a key problem in the link between research and practice as 'the weakened capacity of teachers to engage with research' (let alone one of the elements in Table 12.1: their ability to become involved *in* it). Hannon (1998) talks of the reduction of 'teacher autonomy' as a result of government policies at the end of the last century which were driven by a 'distrust of the profession' (p. 152). Teachers became burdened with a highly prescriptive National Curriculum, vastly increased paperwork and heavy inspection systems to 'ensure compliance'.

In my own experience teacher education courses changed radically in this period. Initial teacher *education* became centrally controlled initial teacher *training* with no room for beginning teachers to even consider research, let alone engage in it. Similarly, in-service courses often became 'how to do it' days with instruction on how to implement the latest initiative or curriculum development such as investigational work (in science) or the 'Literacy Hour'. As Hannon puts it,

> Curricular and pedagogic initiatives at the level of the school or local area are suffocated. Gone are the days of local courses, teachers' centres, active professional organizations, support for masters' level study and the celebration of teacher researchers. Add to this worsened working conditions relating to class sizes and the physical deterioration of schools, and rising levels of stress, and one has to ask how much attention it is reasonable to expect teachers to give to educational research. For practitioners to be engaged *with* research some should ideally be engaged *in* it, and all must have the opportunity to read, reflect upon, discuss and act on research findings. (*Ibid.*, p. 153, my emphasis)

Models of Interaction between Research, Policy and Practice
The climate for educational research therefore changed radically in the 1990s. Prior to the beginning of this era, models had been put forward for the interaction between research findings and policy or practice. Bulmer (1982a), for example, described two main models: the *engineering* model and the *enlightenment* model (pp. 42–9). The engineering model, according to Bulmer, gained ground in the 1970s and received 'unintended impetus' from Karl Popper's faith in the idea of 'piecemeal social engineering'. Bulmer describes the model as

> a linear one. A problem exists; information or understanding is lacking either to generate a solution to the problem or to select

among alternative solutions; research provides the missing knowledge; and a solution is reached. (*Ibid.*, p. 42)

A basic flaw in the model is the assumption that all parties are in agreement about *ends* – research then provides solutions on the *means* to achieving those ends. As we discuss later, in considering the 'is/ ought' distinction, reality is far more complex. Means and ends often become entangled; research can often show what *can* be achieved (even if it cannot determine what ought to be).

Bulmer discusses these and other weaknesses in this model and goes on to describe the enlightenment model. Here the role of the researcher is to create 'the intellectual conditions for problem solving ... by weakening myths and refuting distortions' (Janowitz, 1972, p. 5). As Bulmer (1982a) puts it, policy-makers in this model use research to '*orient* themselves to problems' rather than using it to *solve* specific problems: 'Research provides the intellectual background of concepts, orientations and empirical generalizations that inform policy' (p. 48). Other key terms which characterize the enlightenment model are: 'importance of the social context', and 'rational inquiry and intellectual debate' (Janowitz, 1972); rethinking 'comfortable assumptions', 'social criticism', re-ordering the 'goals and priorities of policy-makers' (Weiss, 1977); 'illumination of opinion', 'commentators and illuminators of the current scene' (Shils, 1961).

These were the views and key terms of authors in the 1960s, 70s and 80s. In the 1990s, Wittrock (1991) was one of the authors who took the idea of different models of interaction a stage further. He suggested eight different models of how 'social knowledge' can interact with 'public policy' (including the two identified by Bulmer). They cannot be considered in full here but, very briefly, the five models which (in my view) relate to educational research are:

1. the *enlightenment* model in which the aim of research is to illuminate problems and issues;
2. the *engineering* model in which social research produces 'neatly delimited bits of input for the decision-making machinery of the policy process' (Wittrock, 1991, p. 338);
3. the *policy-learning* model which views policies as rather like hypotheses which need to be tried out and tested. Researchers are involved in evaluating new policies with the aim of gradually refining and improving them;
4. the *social-problem-solving* model: research knowledge is seen as just one form of knowledge, advice or evidence in helping to solve

social problems; social scientists (or educational researchers) do not have a monopoly on the knowledge and insight relevant to 'policy processes' (Wittrock, 1991, p. 347);

5. the *adversary* model: research knowledge often serves as 'ammunition in partisan battles'. 'Controversy over an issue may well be conducive rather than detrimental to the use of social knowledge' (p. 348). In other words, the presence of controversy or disagreement can often stimulate educational research.

Wittrock devotes an entire chapter to the various models of interaction – the above five points hardly do them justice. However, they are useful in reflecting on the value and the role of educational research. In the present climate no single model could apply (which will please the postmodernists). This is hardly surprising since educational research is a very 'broad church' covering a wide range of people from a range of backgrounds with a range of interests (rather like religion or science). Educational research is not a unified, homogenous activity or pursuit. Like science, it has a range of branches with a range of methods (cf. there is no such thing as *the* scientific method). Educational research can be funded or unfunded, done by teams or individuals, conducted by 'insiders' or outsiders and so on. But elements of each of the five models above can be seen in different types of educational research. For example, the engineering and policy-learning models apply to some of the centrally funded research projects that are sponsored by large organizations such as the DfEE. Bodies responsible for making policy regularly 'put it forward' first, then research or evaluate it second. They often seek 'neatly delimited bits of input' for the process of policy-making, commonly by asking research organizations such as universities to tender for it.

Similarly, the adversary model applies to many activities which come under the umbrella of educational research. Occasionally, adversaries may engage with each other at an academic level, e.g. debates over theories of learning such as constructivism or controversies over the origins of language. At other times the adversaries may appear at a policy level or even at the level of practice. Controversy over practice and policy can fuel, and be fuelled by, educational research.

Other types of educational research may relate more closely to the enlightenment model or perhaps the social-problem-solving model. The long-standing idea of the teacher-as-researcher, and certain aspects of action research, may find some affinity with these models.

In my view the various models are valuable as an aid in reflecting on the purpose of educational research - but not one of them could reflect the complexity of the real world. For example, the enlightenment model is attractive in seeing educational research as 'creating the intellectual conditions for problem solving' and 'shaping the way people think in relation to policy rather than policy itself' (Hargreaves, 1999, p. 243). But to adopt it wholesale could be considered naïve:

> it would be thoroughly unrealistic to adopt an 'enlightenment concept' of the research–practice relationship in which policy-making waits until there is sufficient sound evidence on which to proceed, or professional dilemmas are left unresolved until enough 'facts' are known ... practice and policy will always be powerfully shaped by other considerations than even the best available evidence. (Edwards, 1996, p. 4)

Edwards' pragmatism is surely correct. The history of educational research contains many examples of 'bad' research which has had an impact and 'good' research which has been ignored. The relationship between research, policy and practice is a complex one. No single model will map onto the messy reality. Nisbet and Broadfoot (1980) made this point many years ago when they wrote of the 'complexity of the variables affecting impact' many of which are concerned with the 'characteristics and predilections of the receiving individuals and groups'. This certainly applies to policy-makers and curriculum developers. But it applies just as strongly to practitioners, i.e. teachers at primary, secondary and tertiary level. Fullan (1991) discussed how innovations must pass the 'practicality ethic' of teachers, comprising 'congruence, instrumentality and cost'. Teachers will assess proposed change in terms of their perceptions of its need, clarity, complexity and practicality (to use Fullan's terms). They will, in my view, tend to weigh up educational research using similar criteria.

Osmosis Model
Another model, which some have had an optimistic faith in, is what I will call the 'osmosis model'. This is the idea that educational research somehow permeates or percolates into the discourse, thinking and practice of teachers over a long period, often unnoticed. In the 1970s, Taylor talked of the influence of educational research on 'staffroom conversation' and school decision-making as being 'tenuous and indirect'. Ideas from research 'make their way into thinking and practice less directly – through the literature on education ...

through courses, conferences and lectures' (Taylor, 1973, p. 200). Thus educational research has an influence which is often unacknowledged.

This model is attractive and can certainly be used to boost the self-esteem of researchers. But the success of the osmosis depends entirely on the educational conditions. As mentioned already, the climate of the 1990s was far less conducive to osmosis than the more open and less centrally controlled era of the 1970s.

WHAT CAN BE EXPECTED OF EDUCATIONAL RESEARCH?

This chapter, and other parts of the book, have discussed many of the problems inherent in carrying out educational research (and indeed research of other kinds). The list of challenges or issues includes the difficulties caused by:

1. the inevitable influence of the researcher on the researched (and vice versa);
2. practical and ethical problems of organizing research involving people;
3. the rapidity of change in social situations (events can often 'overtake' research);
4. the complexity involved in replicating previous research;
5. the problem of identifying, isolating and operationalizing the many variables in a real-life situation;
6. the wariness with which generalizations must be made – so that they often become 'particularizations' by successive qualifications.

These are some of the problems present in conducting, analysing and presenting research. Add to this list the complexity of the connection between research, policy and practice:

1. the tenuous, often indirect, connections between them; and the lack of a model which can adequately explain these connections;
2. the fact that research evidence is rarely compelling or influential enough to alter people's views, commitments and values – or policies;
3. the tough 'practicality test' which teachers will apply to research (and this will only occur if they are given the opportunity to engage with it, let alone become involved in it).

Finally, there is the age-old 'is/ought' problem, discussed, most famously, by David Hume. The Scottish philosopher (1711–76) argued that an 'ought' cannot be derived logically from an 'is', i.e.

statements about values and actions (what ought to be done) cannot follow logically from factual statements about what *is* the case. We all make the jump from is to ought – but it is not a logical leap. The jump depends on our views, prejudices, experiences, politics, predilections ... and so on.

The 'ought' statements which determine policies and practices do not follow logically from the 'is' statements, which largely form the substance of research.

So, what hope is there for educational research? How can it have a role and be of value? I would like to finish on an optimistic note by expressing my own views on what should, and should not be, expected of educational research. First, what should not be expected:

1. What should not be expected is that it can provide definitive answers on either policy or practice. Hume's is/ought distinction can be brought to the defence of educational research. Research cannot determine how teachers ought to teach or what policies or curricula ought to be put forward. Policies and practices can be informed by educational research but they cannot be derived from it. Teaching can be 'evidence-informed' (Hargreaves, 1999) but not evidence-based in the sense of being logically derived from it.
2. Research should not be expected to identify direct causal relationships, i.e. doing X causes Y. Even in the physical sciences, a belief in crude causality was abandoned well before the end of the last century. Yet some sort of yearning for causal knowledge still lingers on in the minds of many critics of educational research. They seem to be longing for some sort of *causal agent* to be found by researchers studying teaching and learning. It won't happen.

David Hume, again, talked of this yearning for an identifiable agent. In his essay 'Of the Standard of Taste', Hume discusses a piece of *Don Quixote* wherein are two wine tasters. One describes the wine as 'having a hint of iron', the other finds it 'leathery'. When they open the cask they find at the bottom an iron key on a leather thong. The educational equivalent of Hume's key and thong is the continuing belief that research can establish, objectively, *the* optimum teaching method, *the* optimum curriculum or *the* optimum system of managing institutions at the bottom of the cask.

Many studies in education, particularly those which have attempted to measure the impact of an innovation such as IT, have fallen into the trap of seeking the key on a leather thong. But this search for causal agents has at least four problems:

1. the hidden variables and complexity of most real situations, e.g. free school dinners 'causing' low achievement;
2. direction is often unknown, e.g. do large classes 'cause' higher achievement? – no, it is the other way around in most secondary schools;
3. seeming causality is often just 'constant conjunction' (Hume), e.g. thunder follows lightning but is not caused by it;
4. connections often occur entirely by chance, e.g. size of left foot and IQ.

Educational researchers (and critics of them) should give up the search for the iron key on the leather thong, i.e. causality and causal agents – just as scientists have done. So what should they be expected to provide to the education community? My view is that the sights of educational research should be set realistically but not apologetically:

1. Educational research can provide illumination of and insight into situations, events, issues, policies and practices in education at all levels. A naïve version of the enlightenment model discussed earlier does have its flaws; but the model also has certain strengths in considering the value and purpose of educational research. Research can 'shed light' on educational practices and policies. It can provide

   > an angle of vision, a focus for looking at the world. It is a source of illumination on the rich details and tangled inter-relationships in that world. Whatever else it may or may not do, it serves a global function of enlightenment. (Weiss, 1977, p. 17)

2. Educational research (like many aspects of scientific research) may not be able to show direct causal relationships or identify causal agents. But it can show important connections and correlations. We cannot, for example, state that poverty *causes* low educational achievement. But we can surely say that it is related to it, along with other factors.
3. Finally, a more general purpose for educational research in the future must surely be a continuation of its role as a 'moral witness' (Goodson, 1999) or a critical commentator on initiatives and developments in education. Its value lies in 'keeping watch' on what happens in the fields of curriculum, policy and practice. Researchers are people, and inevitably partisan, but their importance lies in maintaining a 'critical distance' (Wittrock, 1991, p. 351) from events and policies. Mortimore (2000, p. 22) argues that

researchers should 'ask difficult questions' and 'speak up for what we believe is right'. He cites the late Bishop Trevor Huddleston who described universities as the 'eyes of society'.

Educational research in the future will stand a much greater chance of fulfilling its role and meeting these more realistic expectations if three of the recommendations of the 1990s are put into practice: first, the creation of 'public fora' (Hillage *et al.*, 1998) within which researchers, policy-makers and practitioners can work together; secondly, and partly as a result of such fora, research is made more readily available and accessible to 'those who can benefit from it' (Hargreaves, 1999, p. 248); and, finally, if we can return to a climate in which teachers have the time and opportunity to engage with and become involved in educational research (to use Hannon's 1998 ecological metaphor), not as reluctant 'consumers' but as willing participants.

Educational research can bring about improvement, even if this happens by a slow osmotic process. Educational research can make education better. Otherwise, why do it?

Appendix 1: Eight examples of books reporting educational research

Example 1: Beachside Comprehensive: A case study of schooling. Stephen Ball (Cambridge University Press, 1981)

Area:	The first detailed study of a comprehensive school based on the long-term work of a participant observer.
Focus:	Mixed ability and banding in the 'academic' subjects of one school.
Sample:	One comprehensive school for three years (1973–6) chosen for being 'innovative', welcoming and open; selected teachers and mixed-ability classes within that school.
Data collection:	Participant observation (including teaching); documents and files, e.g. school detention book, registers; interviews ranging from taped sessions to informal chats; respondent validation of data, including feedback sessions with groups of teachers; notebook and research diary.
Publication:	Book published five years after the last fieldwork (reduced to 80,000 words from an initial 120,000); journal articles.

Example 2: The Scars of Dyslexia. Janice Edwards (Cassell, 1994)

Focus:	The educational experiences of dyslexic children.

Sample:	Eight 16–17-year-old boys from a special school where the author worked.
Data collection:	Pupil interviews, using a 36-question schedule; systematic analysis of pupils' written work and reading; interviews with parents; documents.
Data analysis:	The case record of each pupil (and subsequent write up) was structured under categories: background story; negative experiences, e.g. humiliation, persecution; associative reactions, e.g. truancy, lack of confidence; Appendix, e.g. work samples, examination results.
	The results from each case were summarized and compared in a separate section, using tables and matrices.
Publication:	MEd thesis (for which the fieldwork was carried out); book for Cassell.

Example 3: Young Children Learning: Talking and thinking at home and school. Barbara Tizard and Martin Hughes (Fontana, 1984)

Focus:	Children's talk at home (with their mother) and at school (with their teacher); **hypothesis:** 'There are important differences in the quality of parent–child and teacher–child dialogues'; **other foci**: the potential of the home as a learning environment, the role of the adult in it and the role of curiosity in the child's learning.
Sample:	Thirty girls (fifteen 'middle-class', fifteen 'working-class'), all three months either side of their fourth birthdays, English-speaking, all at LEA nursery schools in London or Brighton.
Data collection:	Radio microphones (linked to audio recorders) sewn into a specially made tunic/dress ('the special dress') – two children who refused to wear it were dropped from the study; field notes; data collected in 1976–7.
Data analysis:	Tapes transcribed and annotated (average of

nine hours transcription time to one hour of
tape), about 80 pages of A4 per child. Analysed
by:

- coding systems with inter-coder checks;
- talk divided up into 'conversations';
- further qualitative analysis by researchers,
  e.g. looking at 'learning opportunities'.

Publication: Five journal papers (producing 'virtually no
reaction'); one book (a Fontana paperback,
over 24,000 copies sold, producing reaction
from many quarters); short articles for *TES*
and *New Society*.

Example 4: Common Knowledge: The development of understanding in the classroom. Derek Edwards and Neil Mercer (Routledge, 1989)

Focus: Teaching and learning in classrooms.

Questions and aims: How do people teach and learn together? How
is knowledge shared?; to show that Piaget and
followers were largely wrong in ignoring the
communicative aspect of teaching and learning.

Sample: Three groups of five or six pupils aged
between 8 and 11 in three local primary
schools, each working with their usual teacher
on one topic over three consecutive lessons of
40–60 minutes each, i.e. nine lessons in total.

Data collection: (a) observation and video recording (using a
cameraman and sound engineer); (b) inter-
views with teachers and pupils about the
lessons, and the learning and teaching in them.
Outcome: 450 minutes of video and 270
minutes of audio tape.

Data analysis: Transcription of all the discourse, observation
of video tapes adding notes, e.g. on non-verbal
communication, alongside the transcripts; joint
watching and discussion of the video record-
ings, making notes together.

Publication: Aimed at two audiences: the academic community and the 'professional' education community, e.g. teachers. Result: one book, several journal papers.

Example 5: Schooling the Smash Street Kids. Paul Corrigan (Macmillan, 1979)

Area:	The problems of secondary education as experienced by 'bored 15-year-old, working-class boys and by tired exasperated teachers'. (Corrigan confesses to following the 'male-dominated sociological line of researching only into male adolescent activity'.)
Focus:	Five main questions: Why do kids play truant? Why do they muck about in class? Why do they choose dead-end jobs? What do they get out of pop music and football? Why do kids get into trouble on the street?
Sample:	Two 'working-class' secondary schools in Sunderland, 45 boys in one school (questionnaire only), 48 boys in a second school (interview and questionnaire).
Data collection:	Questionnaire to the 93 boys in two schools; tape-recorded interviews in one school; observing; chatting at lunchtimes.
Publication:	PhD thesis at University of Durham; book for Macmillan; articles.

Example 6: Social Relations in a Secondary School. David Hargreaves (Routledge and Kegan Paul, 1967)

Aim:	To provide an analysis of the school as 'a dynamic system of social relations' by making an intensive study of day-to-day behaviour and interaction within the school.
Focus:	Streaming (the informal and formal processes at work); teacher–pupil relationships; delinquency; out-of-school situations – homes, parents, activities.

Sample:	A hundred fourth-year boys, aged 14–15, in their last year of schooling in a secondary modern in a northern industrial town.
Data collection:	Teaching, observing, questionnaire and interviews, informal discussion, i.e. a participant observer for a complete school year.
Publication:	A 226-page book.

Example 7: Learning to Labour: How working class kids get working class jobs. Paul Willis (Saxon House, 1977)

Focus:	The transition from school to work of non-academic, working-class boys in the 1970s.
Sample:	Case study of twelve boys in a secondary modern in an industrial Midlands town, from their penultimate year of school through to the workplace/shopfloor; complemented by comparative studies of five other groups of 'lads', four from different schools of different kinds.
Data collection:	Extensive participant observation, in school and then at work; recorded interviews; group discussions and conversations with pupils; taped conversations with parents, 'senior masters' and junior teachers.
Publication:	Research carried out from 1972 to 1975; book published in 1977.

Example 8: Typical Girls? Young women from school to the job market. Christine Griffin (Routledge and Kegan Paul, 1985)

Area:	An ethnographic study of young women's transitions from school to work carried out by a female researcher (as opposed to 'the numerous male academics who have studied the position of "lads" ' (*Ibid.*, 1985, p. 5).
Focus:	Initial focus: interviews with 180 students in six Birmingham schools, and with head teachers, careers and form teachers. In-depth

study: a group of young women moving from the final year of school into the labour market, examining the influence of family life and gender.

Sample: Twenty-five fifth-formers, leaving school in 1979, mainly white working-class, all with four or less O-levels; ten companies offering 'women's jobs' in office or factory, or 'men's jobs' in engineering.

Data collection: Loosely structured interviewing of initial 180 in groups or individually; for the 25 chosen, interviews, visits to homes, workplace and social life, e.g. pubs; observation in each company, roughly 5–10 days in each. No surveys, questionnaires or computer programs used.

Publication: Book chapters, papers, book published in 1985, six years after first students left school.

Appendix 2: Words to watch when writing

---

1. Singulars ... and plurals
i. **criterion   criteria**
   e.g. 'The main criterion for a good book is readability.'
   e.g. 'The three criteria for a good thesis are structure, clear presentation and grounding in the literature.'

ii. **phenomenon   phenomena**
   e.g. 'The phenomenon of corn circles is fascinating.'
   e.g. 'The world is full of strange phenomena.'

iii. **datum   data**
   (This is a classic mistake in theses.)
   e.g. 'The data were collected by a team from Sussex.' (NB: data = facts)

2. Misused words
i. **effect ... and affect**
   (Affect is a verb meaning to act on, alter or influence.)
   e.g. 'How does the seating in a classroom affect the pupils' working relationships?'

Affect can also mean pretend.
   e.g. 'He affected not to be hurt.'

Effect, as a verb, means to bring about, accomplish or achieve.
   e.g. 'She effected a remarkable change in her students' attitudes.'

Effect, as a noun, can mean result.
   e.g. 'His shouting had no effect.' Or it can mean a state of being operative, e.g. 'She put Plan B into effect.'

The most common mistake is to use effect as a verb instead of affect.
e.g. 'The fall effected him badly', is not correct. The sentence below is ugly, but correct.

'The locals were really affected by the effect of the storm but whilst they affected not to be concerned they quietly put Plan C into effect with an excellent effect.'

ii. principle ... and principal
Principle means a rule, and is a noun.
e.g. 'A guiding principle in football is to kick the ball not the player.'

Principal means the head or the leader.
e.g. 'The principal of a school', or it can mean (as an adjective) main.
e.g. 'The principal principle in cricket is to get the other team out.'

iii. their ... and there
Their is for something belonging to some people or things; **there** is for a place, or to start a sentence.
Correct usage: 'Their bags were left lying over there'; 'There is a flaw in their argument.'

3. Common mis-spellings

arguement for argument
existance for existence
its for it's (and vice versa)
reasearch for research
seperate for separate

grammer for grammar
subsistance for subsistence
independant for independent
dependant for dependent

Example: 'It's true that in Essex there is an independent argument for research into the existence of a separate subsistence fund for its grammar school pupils.'

Appendix 3: Some guidelines on punctuation

Here are some guidelines which may help overcome certain recurrent problems in writing:

1. **Apostrophes to indicate possession**
   Mark a pupil's book. Assess an individual pupil's understanding.
       (These are examples of a *single* person's possessions.)
   Mark ten pupils' books. Assess students' understanding of the topic.
       (These are examples of *several* persons' possessions.)
   Mark James' book. Mark James's book.
       (James's name ends in 's': either of these is acceptable.)
   The women's toilets are on odd-numbered floors. What should I do with the children's money? What colour is your team's kit? Mark a few people's books.
       ('Women', 'children', 'team' and 'people' refer in each case to a *single group*.)
   Wash all the teams' kits.
       (This time the reference is to *several* teams, not just one.)
2. **Its and It's**
   Its: The beaker and its lid are here. The moon is in its orbit.
       ('Its' has no apostrophe when it indicates possession, as in the two examples above.)
   It's cold. Where's the cat – it's not here, is it?
       These *aren't* examples of possession. The apostrophe indicates that there's at least one letter missed out (there could've been several omitted). It's is short for 'it is'.)
3. **Commas, semi-colons and colons**
   • A comma is used to indicate a slight pause in a spoken sentence,

like this. The part of the sentence following the comma may well not make sense as a sentence on its own, as these words show.

- A semi-colon indicates that the spoken pause would have a length between that of a comma and that of a full stop. The part of the sentence that follows a semi-colon would usually make sense as a sentence on its own, as in this example: 'Sheffield Wednesday are playing well at the moment; I think they could beat anyone.'
- The words following a colon often amount to an example or a further explanation of what has gone before; for example, 'This is how you get there: first right, second left, then straight on.'

What do you make of the examples below?
   Here's the cat's food. It'll love it: it's its favourite!
   If the Bunsen's hot, leave it; if it's cold, put it away.

(based on a handout from Jon Scaife)

Glossary of terms used in educational research

a posteriori: coming after; following from and dependent upon experience and observation, i.e. *after* experience.

a priori: coming before; prior to, and independent of, experience or observation, i.e. *before* experience.

action research: a term coined by social psychologist Kurt Lewin (1890–1947) in the 1940s. Lewin suggested the action research 'spiral' of: plan, act, observe, reflect. Action research is usually undertaken by a person who is both the researcher and practitioner/user. For example, researchers might aim to explore how and in what ways certain aspects of their teaching are 'effective'; this research could then inform and improve their current practice.

Carr and Kemmis (1986) argued that all action research has the key features of improvement and involvement: involvement of practitioners in all phases, i.e. planning, acting, observing and reflecting; improvement in the understanding practitioners have of their practice and the practice itself.

applied research: research directed towards solving a problem or designed to provide information that is immediately useful and applicable.

attitude test: a test designed to measure a person's feelings and attitudes toward social situations or people; usually seen as relatively crude measuring instruments.

audiences: individuals, e.g. lecturers/teachers, groups or organizations (e.g. pressure groups, schools) who might use the findings produced by a researcher.

bias: the conscious or sub-conscious influence of a researcher on what and how research is carried out. Bias can/will affect: the choice of topics/problems/questions to research; research planning and design; methods of data collection, e.g. interviewing; data analysis; interpretation of results; discussion and conclusion.

biased sample: the result of a sampling strategy which deliberately includes or excludes certain individuals or groups. A sample may be biased for good reasons (see purposive sampling).

case study: the study of single 'cases' or 'units of analysis', e.g. a person, an event, a group, an organization, a classroom, a town, a family ... Commonly used in law, medicine and education. Howard Becker, the American sociologist, urges that case-study researchers should continually ask: 'What is this a case *of*?' Case study is often chosen to explore how or why questions and situations in their natural setting when the researcher is not attempting to control or intervene in them (Yin, 1984). Cases are often chosen to deepen understanding of an event, a problem, an issue, a theory, a model ... (Stake, 1995).

cognition: the act of knowing or understanding; knowledge can be knowledge *that* or knowledge *how* (Ryle, 1949) and in some cases knowledge *why*. Thus the process of cognition can involve skill, knowledge or understanding.

control group: the group of people (or plants or animals) in an experiment who do not experience the treatment given to an experimental group – allegedly as identical as possible to the experimental group. In theory, the purpose of a control group is to show what would have happened to the experimental group if it had not been exposed to the experimental treatment.

deconstruction: a way of examining texts (i.e. 'taking apart'). By searching for the unspoken or unformulated messages of a text, it can be shown to be saying something more than or different to what it appears or purports to say. Texts say many different things, i.e. there is not one essential meaning (Jacques Derrida, 1967).

dependent variable: the thing/phenomenon which you study or measure in a controlled experiment; the variable changed or influenced by an experimental treatment.

discourse analysis: a general term used to encompass a range of approaches to analysing talk, text, writing etc; mainly concerned with analysing *what* is being communicated and *how*, looking for codes, rules and signs in speech or text.

document analysis: the strategies and procedures for analysing and interpreting the documents of any kind important for the study of a particular area. Documents might be public, e.g. government documents, media cuttings, television scripts, minutes of meetings; or private, e.g. letters, diaries, school records, memoirs, interview transcripts, transcripts prepared from video records or photographs.

empirical research: (as opposed to deskwork or 'armchair' research) inquiry involving first-hand data collection, e.g. by interviewing, observation, questionnaire. People can do empirical research without being 'empiricist' (like 'positivist', a term of abuse).

empiricism: the belief that all reliable knowledge is dependent upon and derived from *sense experience*. The rest is myth, hearsay, witchcraft or metaphysics. (see the Scottish philosopher David Hume, 1711–76). The strict form of empiricism is *logical positivism*, which maintains that the only valid knowledge claims are those which are directly verifiable by sense data. This rules out most social science, the bulk of modern science (including physics), all of theology and metaphysics, ethics and morals, and most theory of any kind. A bit too strict, perhaps, and widely attacked, e.g. Kuhn, Polanyi, the later Wittgenstein.

epistemology: the study of the nature and validity of human knowledge, e.g. the difference between knowledge and belief. The two traditional camps have been: *rationalism*, which stresses the role of human reason in knowing; and *empiricism* which stresses the importance of sensory perception. Immanuel Kant argued that most knowledge is a synthesis or combination of the two approaches.

ethnography: a methodology with its roots in anthropology (literally, the study of people); aims to describe and interpret human behaviour within a certain *culture*; uses extensive fieldwork and participant observation, aiming to develop rapport and empathy with people studied.

experimental group: the group of people in a controlled experiment who experience the experimental treatment or intervention.

formative evaluation: evaluation carried out in the early or intermediate stages of a programme, a course or an intervention while changes can still be made; the formative evaluation shapes and informs those changes. Summative evaluation is carried out at the end of a programme or intervention to assess its impact.

generalizability: the extent to which research findings in one context can be transferred or applied to other contexts or settings. No findings, even those based on a statistical sample, can be generalized with complete certainty.

grounded theory: theory emerging from the data collected in a research study by the process of induction.

Hawthorne effect: initial improvement in performance following any newly introduced change – an effect or problem which researchers need to be wary of if making an intervention into a natural setting, e.g. introducing new teaching methods to assess their impact.

The name is based on a 1924 study of productivity at the Hawthorne factory in Chicago. Two carefully matched groups (experimental and control) were isolated from other factory workers. Factors in the working conditions of the experimental group were varied, e.g. illumination, humidity, temperature, rest periods. No matter what changes were made, including negative ones such as reduced illumination or shorter rest periods, their productivity showed an upward trend. Just as surprisingly, although no changes were made to the conditions of the control group, their output increased steadily.

hermeneutics: the art or science of interpretation, a term first coined by William Dilthey (1833–1911). The term may now apply to the interpretation of a text, a work of art, human behaviour, discourse, documents and so on. Hans-Georg Gadamer (1900–78) proposed hermeneutics as a form of practical philosophy or methodology; the aim is to interpret and understand the meaning of social actions and social settings.

hypothesis: a tentative proposal or unproved theory, put forward for examination and testing; it can be used to guide and direct research along certain lines with certain procedures to 'put the hypothesis to the test'.

induction: the process of inferring a general law from the observation of particular instances. David Hume (1711–76) talked of the 'fallacy of induction': we can never be certain of a general law, e.g. 'All swans are white', based on particular observations, e.g. seeing numerous white swans.

instrument: any technique or tool that a researcher uses, e.g. a questionnaire, an interview schedule, observation framework etc.

interview schedule: a set of questions used in interviewing; questions may range from *closed* to *open*, in which respondents express their views and experiences openly and freely. Interviews may range from unstructured to semi-structured to completely structured (a face-to-face questionnaire), i.e. from totally open to completely predetermined.

interpretative approach: argues that human behaviour can only be explained by referring to the subjective states of the people acting in it; this approach can be applied to the study of social actions/activity and texts or documents; opposed to positivism which claims that social life can only be explained by the examination of observable entities (cf. empiricism).

logical positivism: a philosophy developed between 1922 and 1940 by the 'Vienna Circle' based on the earlier philosophies of Auguste Comte (1798–1857) and the empiricist David Hume (1711–76); argues that the only meaningful knowledge is that based on, and verifiable by, direct sense experience. Hence, any descriptive statement that cannot be empirically verified by sense observation is meaningless. This doctrine would rule out theology, metaphysics and hermeneutics.

Logical positivism is now largely discredited but is often (wrongly) confused with positivism and with 'being scientific'; all three are based on different ideas.

longitudinal research: research in which data are collected and analysed on the same individuals or the same organizations, e.g. schools, colleges or the same groups, e.g. families, at different points over an extended period of time; for example, on a carefully chosen sample of children/youths/adults at the ages of 7, 14, 21, 28, 35, 42 (see Michael Apted's (1999) *7-UP* (London: Heinemann, and related television programmes)).

methodology: the study of the methods, design and procedures used in research.

N: the number of people or subjects studied or sampled in a research project; e.g. N = 1, signifies a single case study.

Ockham's razor (sometimes Occam): after William of Ockham's (1285–1349) law of economy: entities are not to be multiplied beyond necessity. A law originally applied to *ontology* (see entry) but can be usefully stretched further, e.g. chopping excessive words from a paper or thesis.

ontology: the study or theory of 'what is', i.e. the characteristics of reality.

paradigm: a term which became fashionable following Thomas Kuhn's (1922–96) book *The Structure of Scientific Revolutions*; now commonly over-used to mean perspective/view of the world, methodological position, viewpoint, community of researchers, cognitive framework, and so on. In ER, people often speak of 'the qualitative and quantitative paradigms', as if they were separate and mutually exclusive; or the 'positivist paradigm' as a widely held and dangerous tendency (dictionary definitions of paradigm: *pattern, example*).

participant observation: a methodology or practice with its roots in early twentieth-century anthropology; it entails a researcher spending a prolonged period of time participating in the daily activities of a community or a group, e.g. a tribe, a gang, a school, the armed forces; and observing their practices, norms, customs and behaviour (either overtly or covertly). The researcher becomes socialized into the group being studied. The method therefore demands that a fine line be drawn between empathy/rapport with the group and over-familiarity/total involvement.

As a method it may lead to both practical concerns, e.g. safety; and ethical concerns, e.g. pretending to be something you are not, in some situations.

positivism: the belief that all true knowledge is based on observable phenomena (Auguste Comte, 1798–1857) (cf. empiricism: all concepts are derived from experience); NOT the same as 'scientific' which does deal in unobservable, theoretical entities. 'You positivist!' is often used for verbal abuse.

postmodernism: a widely used term, impossible to define, encompassing a broad range of amorphous ideas, e.g. it signals the end of universal truths, totalistic explanations and 'grand narratives' (J. F. Lyotard, 1984), giving way to little narratives (*petits récits*) and local knowledge, adequate for particular communities. Key words are: difference, heterogeneity, fragmentation and indeterminacy.

purposive/purposeful sampling: sampling done with deliberate aims in mind as opposed to a random sample or one chosen purely for its convenience and accessibility. Cases or sites may be chosen purposefully for a variety of reasons, e.g. for being typical or extreme or deviant or unique or exemplary or revelatory ... Thus cases or sites are selected with certain criteria in mind.

qualitative: of or relating to quality or kind ('qualis' [Greek]); adjective describing methods or approaches which deal with non-numeric data, i.e. words rather than numbers.

quantitative: of quantity or number; methods or approaches which deal with numeric data, amounts or measurable quantities, i.e. numbers. A false dichotomy is often drawn between a qualitative and a quantitative 'paradigm', as if the two approaches could not be used to complement and enrich each other. Also, use of quantitative data is often (wrongly) labelled 'positivism'.

random sample: sample of the members of a given population drawn in such a way that every member of that population has an equal chance of being selected, e.g. every tenth name in a long list. Random sampling should eliminate the operation of bias in selecting a sample. The term 'population' means the entire group from which the sample is selected, e.g. every student in a particular school/college. The population itself depends on the focus and scope of the research.

reflexivity: introspection and self-examination, i.e. the act of reflecting upon and evaluating one's own impact on the situation being studied; also involves researchers in examining their own assumptions, prior experience and bias in conducting the research and analysing its findings.

reliability: commonly used to describe a test or examination. The term is also used in connection with research methods in order to estimate the degree of confidence in the data. Reliability refers to the extent to which a test or technique functions consistently and accurately by yielding the same results at different times or when used by different researchers.

Research is said to be reliable if it can be repeated or replicated by another researcher and/or at a different time.

sample: the smaller number of cases, units or sites selected from a much larger population. Some samples are assumed to be representative of the entire population, i.e. generalizable from, but this can never be done with certainty.

theory: an idea, model or principle used to explain why observed phenomena happen as they do; theory seeks patterns, relationships, correlations, associations or connections, e.g. between aspects of behaviour and factors which might affect it or explain it.

Some theories may be predictive, i.e. capable of predicting certain outcomes given certain factors or circumstances, as well as explanatory. For example, poverty might be a good 'predictor' of low educational achievement (though few would say it *causes* low achievement).

The search for and belief in direct causality, i.e. X causes Y, is now highly debatable in modern science and in ER.

triangulation: the business of giving strength or support to findings/conclusions by drawing on evidence from other sources: (i) other methods (methodological triangulation), e.g. interviews, observations, questionnaires; (ii) other researchers; (iii) other times, e.g. later in a project; (iv) other places, e.g. different regions.

Thus the same area of study is examined from more than one vantage point, cf. surveying a site.

trustworthiness: a criterion offered by Lincoln and Guba (1985) as an alternative to the traditional 'reliability' and 'validity' in judging ER. Trustworthiness has four parts: (i) credibility; (ii) transferability (cf. *external validity*); (iii) dependability; (iv) confirmability (the latter two being parallel to reliability).

validity: the extent or degree to which an inquiry, a method, test, technique or instrument measures what it sets out or purports to measure, e.g. an intelligence test, an interview, a questionnaire. No instrument could ever be said to be valid with total certainty.

External validity is the extent to which the findings or conclusions of a piece of research could be generalized to apply to contexts/situations other than those in which the data have been collected.

Validity can be seen as a measure of the confidence in, credibility of or plausibility of a piece of research.

variable: a measurable or non-measurable characteristic which varies from one individual or organization to another. Some may be qualitative, others quantitative, i.e. expressible as numbers. Age, gender, ability, personality characteristics, 'intelligence' are a few examples of human variables. In some approaches, the researcher attempts to control or manipulate variables; in other approaches the researcher studies or observes them in their natural setting without deliberately intervening.

References and further reading

Allport, G. (1947) *The Use of Personal Documents in the Psychological Sciences.* New York: Social Science Research Council.

Altman, D. G. (1994) 'The scandal of poor medical research'. *British Medical Journal*, **308**, 283–4.

Anderson, B. (1990) *Methodological Errors in Medical Research.* Oxford: Blackwell.

Anderson, G. (1990) *Fundamentals of Educational Research.* Basingstoke: Falmer Press.

Angell, R. C. and Freedman, R. (1953) 'The use of documents, records, census materials and indices', in L. Festinger and D. Katz *Research Methods in the Behavioural Sciences* (1st edn). New York: Holt, Rinehart and Winston, ch. 7, pp. 300–26.

Armstrong, M. (1980) *Closely Observed Children.* London: Writers and Readers.

Ary, D., Jacobs, L. C. and Razavieh, A. (1985) *Introduction to Research in Education* (3rd edn). New York: Holt, Rinehart and Winston.

Atkinson, J. (1968) *The Government Social Survey: A Handbook for Interviewers.* London: HMSO.

Atkinson, P. and Delamont, S. (1985) 'Bread and dreams or bread and circuses? A critique of "case study" research in education', in M. Shipman (ed.) *Educational Research, Principles, Policies and Practices.* London: Falmer Press. (A useful, critical look at case study research, including a strong critique of Simons, 1981, cited below.)

Atkinson, R. (1998) *The Life Story Interview.* London: Sage.

Baker, M. (1994) 'Media coverage of education'. *British Journal of Educational Studies*, **42**(3), 286–97.

Ball, S. J. (1981) *Beachside Comprehensive.* Cambridge: Cambridge University Press.

Ball, S. J. (1990) 'Self-doubt and soft data: social and technical trajectories in ethnographic fieldwork'. *Qualitative Studies in Education*, 3(2), 157–71.

Bassey, M. (1990) 'On the nature of research in education, part I'. *Research Intelligence* (BERA Newsletter), no. 36, pp. 35–8. (See also Bassey's part II and part III articles in *Research Intelligence*, autumn 1990 and winter 1991, nos 37 and 38.)

Becker, H. S. (1970) *Sociological Work: Method and Substance.* Chicago: Aldine.

Becker, H. S. (1986) *Writing for Social Scientists.* Chicago: Chicago University Press.

Bell, J. (1993) *Doing Your Research Project: A Guide for First-time Researchers in Education and Social Science.* Buckingham: Open University Press. (A concise, valuable guide for new researchers, now in its 3rd edition.)

BERA (1992) *Ethical Guidelines for Educational Research.* Edinburgh: British Educational Research Association.

Best, J. W. (1981) *Research in Education* (4th edn). New Jersey: Prentice-Hall.

Best, J. and Kahn, J. V. (1986) *Research in Education* (5th edn). New Jersey: Prentice-Hall.

Bogdan, R. and Biklen, S. (1982) *Qualitative Research for Education.* Boston: Allyn and Bacon.

Bonnett, A. (1993) 'Contours of crisis: anti-racism and reflexivity', in P. Jackson and J. Penrose (eds) *Construction of 'Race', Place and Nation.* London: UCL Press.

Borg, W. R. and Gall, M. D. (1989) *Educational Research: An Introduction.* New York: Longman.

Brenner, M., Brown, J. and Canter, D. (eds) (1985) *The Research Interview: Uses and Approaches.* London: Academic Press.

Bulmer, M. (1979) *Beginning Research.* Milton Keynes: Open University Press.

Bulmer, M. (1982a) *The Uses of Social Research.* Lonson: George Allen & Unwin.

Bulmer, M. (ed.) (1982) *Social Research Ethics: An Examination of the Merits of Covert Participant Observation.* London: Macmillan.

Burgess, R. G. (1981) 'Keeping a research diary'. *Cambridge Journal of Education,* **11**(1), 75–83.

Burgess, R. G. (1982a) 'The unstructured interview as a conversation', in R. G. Burgess (ed.) *Field Research: A Sourcebook and Field Manual.* London: Allen and Unwin.

Burgess, R. G. (ed.) (1982b) *Field Research: A Sourcebook and Field Manual.* London: Allen and Unwin. (The companion volume to the above text consisting of readings on all phases of the research activity.)

Burgess, R. G. (1983) *Experiencing Comprehensive Education.* Methuen.

Burgess, R. G. (1984) *In the Field: An Introduction to Field Research.* London: Allen and Unwin. (One of the most widely cited books on fieldwork, it covers the main issues and problems involved in the 'field' research approach.)

Burgess, R. G. (ed.) (1984) *The Research Process in Educational Settings: Ten Case Studies.* Lewes: Falmer Press. (Ten 'first person accounts' of real-life research.)

Burgess, R. G. (ed.) (1985a) *Strategies of Educational Research: Qualitative Methods.* London: Falmer Press.

Burgess, R. G. (ed.) (1985b) *Field Methods in the Study of Education.* Lewes: Falmer Press.

Burgess, R. G. (1989) (ed.) *The Ethics of Educational Research.* London: Falmer Press.

Capra, F. (1983) *The Tao of Physics.* London: Fontana.

Carr, W. and Kemmis, S. (1986) *Becoming Critical: Education, Knowledge and Action Research.* Lewes: Falmer Press.

Chalmers, A. F. (1982) *What Is This Thing Called Science?* Milton Keynes: Open University Press.

Clifford, G. (1973) 'A history of the impact of research on teaching', in R.

Travers, (ed.) *Second Handbook of Research on Teaching*. Chicago: Rand McNally.

Codd, J. (1988) 'The construction and de-construction of educational policy documents'. *Journal of Educational Policy*, 3(3), 235–47.

Coffey, A. and Atkinson, P. (1996) *Making Sense of Qualitative Data*. London: Sage.

Cohen, L. and Manion, L. (1980) *Research Methods in Education* London: Croom Helm.

Cohen, L. and Manion, L. (1994) *Research Methods in Education* (4th edn). London: Routledge.

Collins, H. (1985) *Changing Order: Replication and Induction in Scientific Practice*. London: Sage.

Cordingley, P. (1999) 'Teachers and research'. *Forum*, **41**(3), 124–5.

Corey, S. (1953) *Action Research to Improve School Practices*. New York: Columbia University.

Dean, J. P. and Whyte, W. (1969) 'How do you know if the informant is telling the truth?', in G. McCall and J. Simmons (eds) *Issues in Participant Observation*. Reading, Mass.: Addison-Wesley.

Delamont, S. (1992) *Fieldwork in Educational Settings*. Basingstoke: Falmer Press.

Denscombe, M. (1998) *The Good Research Guide*. Buckingham: Open University Press.

Denzin, N. (1970) *The Research Act*. Chicago: Aldine.

Denzin, N. and Lincoln, Y. (1994) *Handbook of Qualitative Research*. London: Sage.

Derrida, J. (1978) *Writing and Difference*. London: Routledge.

Dickey, J. W. and Watts, T. (1978) *Analytic Techniques in Urban and Regional Planning*. New York: McGraw Hill.

Douglas, J. (1985) *Creative Interviewing*. Calif.: Sage.

Edwards, D. and Mercer, N. (1993) *Common Knowledge*. London: Routledge.

Edwards, T. (1996) *The Research Base of Effective Teacher Education*. Paper presented at the UCET/OFSTED Conference, 10–11 May.

Eichler, M. (1988) *Nonsexist Research Methods: A Practical Guide*. London: Hyman. (Puts forward a well-argued 'guide' to identifying and eliminating sexist bias in educational research.)

Faraday, A. and Plummer, K. (1979) 'Doing life histories'. *Sociological Review*, 27(4), 773–98.

Farrell, E., Peguero, G., Lindsey, R. and White, R. (1988) 'Giving voice to high school students: pressure and boredom, ya know what I'm saying?' *American Educational Research Journal*, 25(4), 489–502.

Faulkner, R. (1982) 'Improvising on a triad', in J. van Maanen *Variations of Qualitative Research*. Calif.: Sage, pp. 65–102.

Fetterman, D. (ed.) (1984) *Ethnography in Educational Evaluation*. London: Sage.

Feyerabend, P. (1993) *Against Method*. London: Verso.

Fielding, N. (1981) *The National Front*. London: Routledge.

Fielding, N. and Lee, R. (eds) (1991) *Using Computers in Qualitative Research*. London: Sage.

Fink, A. (1995) *How to Ask Survey Questions*. London: Sage.

Flynn, J. R. (1980) *Race, IQ and Jensen*. London: Routledge and Kegan Paul.

Fowles, J. (1976) 'An overview of social forecasting procedures'. *Journal of the American Institute of Planners*, **42**, 253–63.

Frankfort-Nachmias, C. and Nachmias, D. (1992) *Research Methods in the Social Sciences* (4th edn). London: Edward Arnold.

Fullan, M. (1991) *The New Meaning of Educational Change*. London: Cassell.

Gardner, H. (1983) *Frames of Mind: The Theory of Multiple Intelligences*. New York: Basic Books.

Gay, L. R. (1981) *Educational Research: Competencies for Analysis and Application* (2nd edn). Ohio: Charles E. Merrill.

Giddens, A. (1976) *The New Rules of Sociological Method*. London: Hutchinson.

Giles, K. and Hedge, N. (eds) (1994) *The Manager's Good Study Guide*. Milton Keynes: Open University.

Gill, J. and Johnson, P. (1997) *Research Methods for Managers*. London: Paul Chapman.

Gilroy, D. P. (1980) 'The empirical researcher as philosopher'. *British Journal of Teacher Education*, 6(3), 237–50.

Glaser, B. and Strauss, A. (1967) *The Discovery of Grounded Theory*. London: Weidenfeld and Nicholson.

Gleick, J. (1988) *Chaos: Making a New Science*. London: Heinemann.

Goertz, J. and Le Compte, M. (1981) 'Ethnographic research and the problem of data reduction'. *Anthropology and Education Quarterly*, 12, 51–70.

Goertz, J. and Le Compte, M. (1984) *Ethnography and Qualitative Design in Educational Research*. Orlando: Academic Press.

Goffman, E. (1961) *Asylums*. New York: Doubleday.

Gomm, R. and Woods, P. (eds) (1993) *Educational Research in Action*. London: Paul Chapman

Goodson, I. (1999) 'The educational researcher as a public intellectual'. *British Educational Research Journal*, 25(3), 277–97.

Guidford, J. (1967) *The Nature of Human Intelligence*. New York: McGraw-Hill.

Halpin, D. and Troyna, B. (eds) (1994) *Researching Educational Policy: Ethical and Methodological Issues*. London: Falmer Press.

Hammersley, M. (1987) 'Some notes on the terms "validity" and "reliability" '. *British Educational Research Journal*, 13(1), 73–83.

Hammersley, M. (ed.) (1993) *Educational Research: Current Issues*. London: Paul Chapman.

Hammersley, M. (1995) *The Politics of Social Research*. London: Sage.

Hammersley, M. (1997) 'Educational research and teaching: a response to David Hargreaves' TTA lecture'. *British Educational Research Journal*, 23(2), 141–61.

Hammersley, M. and Atkinson, P. (1983) *Ethnography: Principles in Practice*. London: Tavistock.

Hannon, P. (1998) 'An ecological perspective on educational research', in J. Rudduck and D. McIntyre (eds) *Challenges for Educational Research*. London: Paul Chapman.

Harding, S. (ed.) (1987) *Feminism and Methodology*. Milton Keynes: Open University Press. (A collection of readings on feminist research methods.)

Hargreaves, A. (1994) *Changing Teachers, Changing Times*. London: Cassell.

Hargreaves, D. H. (1967) *Social Relations in a Secondary School*. Routledge and Kegan Paul.

Hargreaves, D. H. (1996) *Teaching as a Research-Based Profession: Possibilities and Prospects*. Teacher Training Agency Annual Lecture 1996. London: TTA.

Hargreaves, D. H. (1999) 'Revitalising educational research: lessons from the past and proposals for the future.' *Cambridge Journal of Education,* 29(2), 239–49.

Harrison, D. (1999) 'A guide to using bibliographies, abstracts and indexes' in M. Scarrott (ed.) *Sport, Leisure and Tourism Information Sources.* Oxford: Heinemann.

Heisenberg, W. (1958) *The Physicist's Conception of Nature.* London: Hutchinson.

Helmer, O. (1972) 'On the future state of the Union'. *Report 12–27.* Menlo Park, Calif.: Institute for the Future.

Hillage, J., Pearson, R., Anderson, A. and Tamkin, P. (1998) *Excellence in Research on Schools.* London: DfEE.

Hockey, J. (1991) *Squaddies.* Exeter: Exeter University Press.

Holdaway, S. (1985) *Inside the Police Force.* Oxford: Basil Blackwell.

Howard, K. and Sharp, J. (1983) *The Management of a Student Research Project.* Aldershot: Gower.

Janowitz, M. (1972) *Sociological Models and Social Policy.* Morristown, NJ: General Learning Systems.

Jensen, A. R. (1973) *Educability and Group Differences.* London: Methuen.

Kaplan, A. (1973) *The Conduct of Inquiry.* Aylesbury: Intertext Books.

Karier, C. (1973) 'Ideology and evaluation: In quest of meritocracy'. Paper presented to the Wisconsin conference on education and evaluation, School of Education, University of Wisconsin, Madison, Wisconsin, April 26–27.

Kimmel, A. J. (1988) *Ethics and Values in Applied Social Research.* Newbury Park and London: Sage.

Kluckhohn, C. and Murray, H. A. (eds) (1948) *Personality in Nature, Society and Culture.* New York: Alfred A. Knopf.

Krippendorf, K. (1980) *Content Analysis.* London: Sage.

Krueger, R. (1994) *Focus Groups: A Practical Guide for Applied Research.* Calif.: Sage. (The most detailed book I know on the conduct of focus group research, its value and the issues around it; clearly written; numerous practical points and guidance.)

Kuhn, T. S. (1970) *The Structure of Scientific Revolutions.* Chicago: University of Chicago Press.

Lacey, C. (1970) *Hightown Grammar.* Manchester: Manchester University Press.

Logemann, E. (1997) 'Contested terrain: a history of educational research in the United States 1890–1990'. *Educational Researcher* 26(9), 5–17.

Lakin, S. and Wellington, J. J. (1994) ' "Who will teach the nature of science?": teachers' views of science and their implications for science education'. *International Journal of Science Education,* 16(2), 175–90.

Lakoff, G. and Johnson, M. (1980) *Metaphors We Live By.* Chicago: University of Chicago Press. (A classic text on how metaphors have become embedded and unnoticed in everyday life, thought and language.)

Lather, P. (1986) 'Research as praxis'. *Harvard Educational Review,* 56, 257–77.

Latour, B. and Woolgar, S. (1979) *Laboratory Life: The Social Construction of Scientific Facts.* London: Sage.

Lave, J. (1986) *Cognition in Practice.* Cambridge: Cambrige University Press.

Layder, D. (1993) *New Strategies in Social Research.* Cambridge: Polity Press.

Le Compte, M. and Goertz, J. (1984) 'Ethnographic data collection in education research', 37–59, in Fetterman, D. (ed.) (1994).

Le Compte, M. and Preissle, J. (1984) *Ethnography and Qualitative Design in Educational Research.* London: Academic Press.

Lewin, K. (1946) 'Action research and minority problems'. *Journal of Social Issues,* 2(34–6), 286.

Li, X. and Crane, N. (1993) *Electronic Style: A Guide to Citing Electronic Information.* London: Meckler.

Lincoln, Y. S. and Guba, E. G. (1985) *Naturalistic Inquiry.* Newbury Park and London: Sage.

Locke, J. (1690) (ed. A. D. Woozley, 1964) *An Essay Concerning Human Understanding.* London: Fontana.

Lyotard, J. F. (1984) *The Postmodern Condition: A Report on Knowledge.* Minnesota: University of Minnesota Press.

McNiff, J. (1992) *Action Research: Principles and Practice.* London: Routledge. (Good summary by a former secondary deputy head.)

Maykut, P. and Morehouse, R. (1994) *Beginning Qualitative Research: A Philosophic and Practical Guide.* London: Falmer Press.

Medawar, P. (1963) 'Is the scientific paper a fraud?'. *The Listener,* September.

Medawar, P. (1979) *Advice to a Young Scientist.* New York: Harper and Row.

Merton, R., Fiske, M. and Kendall, P. (1956) *The Focused Interview: A Manual of Problems and Procedures.* Illinois: Free Press.

Miles, M. B. and Huberman, A. M. (1984) *Qualitative Data Analysis: A Sourcebook of New Methods.* Newbury Park, Calif. and London: Sage. (An excellent and imaginative book on different ways of analysing qualitative data.)

Miles, M. B. and Huberman, A. (1994) *Qualitative Data Analysis: An Expanded Sourcebook* (2nd edn). Newbury Park, Calif. and London: Sage.

Mishler, E. (1986) *Research Interviewing: Context and Narrative.* London: Harvard University Press.

Mitchell, J. C. (1983) 'Case and situation analysis'. *Sociological Review,* 31(2), 187–211.

Morgan, D. (1988) *Focus Groups as Qualitative Research.* Newbury Park, Calif. and London: Sage. (Short guide to the conduct and applications of focus groups.)

Mortimore, P. (2000) 'Does educational research matter?' *British Educational Research Journal,* 26(1), 5–24.

Moser, C. A. (1958) *Survey Methods in Social Investigation.* London: Heinemann.

Mouly, G. (1978) *Educational Research: The Art and Science of Investigation.* Boston: Allyn and Bacon.

Neuman, L. W. (1994) *Social Research Methods* (2nd edn). Boston, Mass.: Allyn and Bacon.

Nisbet, J. and Broadfoot, P. (1980) *The Impact of Research on Policy and Practice in Education.* Aberdeen: Aberdeen University Press.

Nisbet, J. and Entwistle, N (1970) *Educational Research Methods.* London: University of London Press.

Nixon, J. (ed.) (1981) *A Teacher's Guide to Action Research.* London: Grant McIntyre.

Nunan, D. (1992) *Research Methods in Language Learning.* Cambridge: Cambridge University Press.

Oppenheim, A. N. (1966) *Introduction to Qualitative Research Methods*. London: Wiley.

Parsons, D. (1984) *Employment and Manpower Surveys: A Practitioner's Guide*. Aldershot: Gower.

Patrick, J. (1973) *A Glasgow Gang Observed*. London: Eyre-Methuen.

Patton, M. (1990) *Qualitative Evaluation and Research Methods*. Newbury Park, Calif.: Sage.

Payne, S. L. (1951) (paperback edn, 1980) *The Art of Asking Questions*. Princeton, NJ: Princeton University Press. (An amusing guide aimed at stopping people from asking silly questions.)

Perry, W. (1970) *Forms of Intellectual and Ethical Development in the College Years*. New York: Holt, Rinehart and Winston.

Peters, R. S. and White, J. P. (1969) 'The philosopher's contribution to educational research'. *Educational Philosophy and Theory*, **1**, 1–15.

Pettigrew, M. and MacLure, M. (1997) 'The press, public knowledge and the grant maintained schools policy'. *British Journal of Educational Studies*, **45**(4), 392–405.

Piaget, J. (1929) *The Child's Conception of the World*. London: Routledge and Kegan Paul.

Platt, J. (1981a) 'Evidence and proof in documentary research:1'. *Sociological Review*, **29**(1), 31–52.

Platt, J. (1981b) 'Evidence and proof in documentary research:2'. *Sociological Review*, **29**(1), 53–66.

Plummer, K. (1983) *Documents of Life: An Introduction to the Problems and Literature of a Humanistic Method*. London: George Allen and Unwin.

Polanyi, M. (1967) *The Tacit Dimension*. Chicago: The University of Chicago Press.

Popper, K. (1963) *Conjectures and Refutations: The Growth of Scientific Knowledge*. London: Routledge and Kegan Paul.

Powney, J. and Watts, M. (1987) *Interviewing in Educational Research*. London: Routledge and Kegan Paul.

Rice, S. A. (ed.) (1931) *Methods in Social Science*. Chicago: University of Chicago Press. (One of the early books describing focus group research in social science.)

Richardson, L. (1985) *The New Other Woman: Contemporary Single Women in Affairs with Married Men*. New York: Free Press.

Richardson, L. (1987) 'Disseminating research to pupilar audiences: the book tour'. *Qualitative Sociology*, **19**(2), 164–76.

Richardson, L. (1990) *Writing Strategies: Reaching Diverse Audiences*. London: Sage.

Richardson, S., Dohrenwend, B. and Klein, D. (1965) *Interviewing: Its Forms and Functions*. New York: Basic Books.

Riley, J. (1990) *Getting the Most from your Data: A Handbook of Practical Ideas on How to Analyse Qualitative Data*. Bristol: Technical and Educational Services Ltd.

Roberts, M. (1996) 'Case study research', in M. Williams (ed.) (1996) *Understanding Geographical and Environmental Education*. London: Cassell, pp. 135–49.

Robson, C. (1993) *Real World Research: A Resource for Social Scientists and Practitioner-Researchers*. Oxford: Basil Blackwell. (A 510-page resource covering almost everything from design to data collection and 'making an impact'.)

Roizen, J. and Jepson, M. (1985) *Degrees for Jobs: Employers' Expectations of Higher Education*. Windsor: SRHE/NFER–Nelson.

Rowland, S. (1984) *The Enquiring Classroom*. Lewes: Falmer Press.

Rubin, H. and Rubin, I. (1995) *Qualitative Interviewing: The Art of Hearing Data*. London: Sage.

Rudduck, J. (1985) 'A case for case records? A discussion of some aspects of Lawrence Stenhouse's work in case study methodology', in R. G. Burgess (ed.) (1985a), pp. 101–19.

Ryle, G. (1949) *The Concept of Mind*. London: Hutchinson.

Sackman, H. (1976) 'A sceptic at the oracle'. *Futures*, 8, 444–6.

Sanger, J., Willson, J., Davis, B. and Whittaker, R. (1997) *Young Children, Videos and Computer Games*. London: Falmer Press.

Schatzman, L. and Strauss, A. (1973) *Field Research: Strategies for a Natural Sociology*. Englewood Cliffs, NJ: Prentice-Hall.

Schon, D. (1971) *Beyond the Stable State*. London: Temple Smith.

Schon, D. (1983) *The Reflective Practitioner*. London: Temple Smith.

Schratz, M. (ed.) (1993) *Qualitative Voices in Educational Research*. London: Falmer Press.

Scott, D. and Usher, R. (eds) (1996) *Understanding Educational Research*. London: Routledge.

Scott, D. and Usher, R. (1999) *Researching Education: Data, Methods and Theory in Educational Inquiry*. London: Cassell.

Scott, J. (1990) *A Matter of Record: Documentary Sources in Social Research*. Cambridge: Polity Press.

Shayer, M. and Adey, P. (1981) *Towards a Science of Science Teaching*. London: Heinemann.

Shils, E. (1961) 'The calling of sociology', in T. Parsons, E. Shils, K. D. Naegele and J. R. Pitts (eds) *Theories of Society*. New York: Free Press, 1405–8.

Shipman, M. (1988) *The Limitations of Social Research* (3rd edn). Harlow: Longman. (A critical look at social science research, discussing issues like reliability, generalizability, validity and 'credibility'.)

Shulman, L. (1987) 'Knowledge and teaching: foundations of the new reforms'. *Harvard Educational Review*, 57(1), 1–22.

Silverman, D. (1993) *Interpreting Qualitative Data: Methods for Analysing Talk, Text and Interaction*. London: Sage. (Concentrates on the study of language in qualitative research by discussing the analysis of interviews, texts and transcripts.)

Simons, H. (1981) *Towards a Science of the Singular: Essays About Case Study in Educational Research and Evaluation*. CARE occasional paper, no.10. Centre for Applied Research in Education, University of East Anglia. (A set of papers presenting what was then a new approach to educational research.)

Simons, H. (1989) 'Ethics of case study in educational research and evaluation', in R. G. Burgess (ed.) *The Ethics of Educational Research*. London: Falmer Press.

Skilbeck, M. (1983) 'Lawrence Stenhouse: research methodology'. *British Educational Research Journal*, **9**(1), 11–20.

Smith, J. M. (1972) *Interviewing in Market and Social Research*. London: Routledge and Kegan Paul.

Sparkes, A. (1994) 'Life histories and the issue of voice: reflections on an emerging relationship'. *Qualitative Studies in Education*, **1**(2), 165–83.

Spindler, G. D. (ed.) (1982) *Doing the Ethnography of Schooling: Educational Anthropology in Action*. New York: Holt, Reinhart and Winston.

Spradley, J. P. (1979) *The Ethnographic Interview*. New York: Holt, Rhinehart and Winston.

Spradley, J. P. (1980) *Participant Observation*. New York: Holt, Rhinehart and Winston.

Stake, R. E. (1994) 'Case Studies', in N. Denzin and Y. Lincoln *Handbook of Qualitative Research*. London: Sage.

Stake, R. (1995) *The Art of Case Study Research*. London: Sage.

Stenhouse, L. (1975) *An Introduction to Curriculum Research and Development*. London: Heinemann.

Stenhouse, L. (1978) 'Case study and case records: towards a contemporary history of education'. *British Educational Research Journal*, **4**(2), 21–39.

Stenhouse, L. (1979) 'The problem of standards in illuminative research'. *Scottish Educational Review*, 11 January.

Stenhouse, L. (1984) 'Library access, library use and user education in sixth forms: an autobiographical account', in R. J. Burgess (ed.) *The Research Process in Educational Settings: Ten Case Studies*. Lewes: Falmer Press, pp. 211–33.

Stenhouse, L. (1985) 'A note on case study and educational practice', in R. G. Burgess (ed.) (1985b), pp. 263–71.

Suppes, P. (ed.) (1978) *Impact of Research on Education: Some Case Studies*. Washington, DC: National Academy of Education.

Taylor, W. (1973) 'Knowledge and research', in W. Taylor (ed.) *Research Perspectives in Education*. London: Routledge and Kegan Paul.

Taylor, S. and Bogdan, R. (1984) *Introduction to Qualitative Research Methods*. New York: Wiley.

Terman, L. M. (1931) 'The gifted child', in C. Murchison (ed.) *A Handbook of Child Psychology*. Worcester, Mass.: Clark University Press.

Tesch, R. (1990) *Qualitative Research: Analysis Types and Software Tools*. London: Falmer Press.

Thorndike, E. L. (1918) 'The nature, purpose and general methods of measurement of educational products'. *Seventeenth Yearbook of the National Society for the Study of Education. Part II. The Measurement of Educational Products*. Bloomington, Illinois: Public School Publishing Company.

Tooley, J. and Darby, D. (1998) *Educational Research: A Critique: A Survey of Published Educational Research*. London: Office for Standards in Education.

Tripp, D. (1993) *Critical Incidents in Teaching*. London: Routledge.

Troyna, B. (1994) 'Reforms, research and being reflective about being reflexive', in Halpin and Troyna (eds).

Turkle, S. (1984) *The Second Self*. London: Granada.

Usher, R. (1996) 'Textuality and reflexivity', in D. Scott and R. Usher (eds).

Usher, R. and Edwards, R. (1994) *Postmodernism and Education*. London: Routledge.

Verma, G. and Mallick, K. (1999) *Researching Education: Perspectives and
Techniques*. London: Falmer Press.

Walford, G. (ed.) (1991) *Doing Educational Research*. London: Routledge. (A set
of semi-autobiographical accounts from thirteen well-known researchers
in education, including Ball, Mac an Ghaill and Tizard and Hughes, in
which they reflect on the problems, methods, publication and impact of
their own particular projects/studies.)

Walford, G. and Miller, H. (1991) *City Technology College*. Buckingham: Open
University Press.

Walker, R. (1980) 'The conduct of educational case studies: ethics, theory and
procedures', in W. B. Dockrell and D. Hamilton (eds) *Rethinking Educational Research*. London: Hodder and Stoughton.

Walker, R. (1985a) *Doing Research: A Handbook for Teachers*. London: Methuen.
(Practical and readable.)

Walker, R. (ed.) (1985b) *Applied Qualitative Research*. Aldershot: Gower. (Collection of readings on qualitative methods, taking a practical approach.)

Walker, R. and Adelman, C. (1972) *Towards a Sociography of Classrooms*. Final
Report. London: Social Science Research Council.

Warburton, T. and Saunders, M. (1996) 'Representing teachers' professional
culture through cartoons'. *British Journal of Educational Studies*. **43**(3), 307–
25.

Watson, F. (1953) 'Research in the physical sciences'. *Phi Delta Kappan*,
Bloomington: Indiana.

Webb, R. (ed.) (1990) *Practitioner Research in the Primary School*. London: Falmer
Press. (Collection of personal accounts of research done by practitioners in
primary schools.)

Webb, S. and Webb, B. (1932) *Methods of Social Study*. London: Longman Green
& Co.

Weiss, C. (ed.) (1977) *Using Social Research in Public Policy Making*. Farnborough:
Saxon House.

Wellington, J. J. (1989) *Education for Employment: The Place of Information
Technology*. Windsor: NFER-Nelson.

Wellington, J. J. (ed.) (1993) *The Work Related Curriculum*. London: Kogan Page.

Wellington, J. J. (ed.) (1998) *Practical Work in School Science: Which Way Now?*
London: Routledge.

Whyte, W. F. (1943) *Street Corner Society: The Social Structure of an Italian Slum*.
Chicago: University of Chicago Press. (Oft-quoted study by an 'upper
middle-class' Harvard researcher who spent an extended period, in the
late 1930s, in the Italian quarter of an 'Eastern City', chosen because it 'best
fitted my picture of what a slum district should look like'! Written almost
like a novel; focuses mainly on the males of the society, their groups,
politics and racketeering.)

Willis, P. (1977) *Learning to Labour: How Working Class Kids Get Working Class
Jobs*. Farnborough: Saxon House.

Wittrock, B. (1991) 'Social knowledge and public policy: eight models of
interaction', in P. Wagner, C. H. Weiss, B. Wittrock and H. Wollman (eds)
Social Sciences and Modern States. Cambridge: Cambridge University Press.

Wolcott, H. F. (1995) *The Art of Fieldwork*. London: Sage Publications.

Woodhead, C. (1997) 'Inspecting schools: the key to raising standards'. Lecture to the Royal Geographical Society, London, 21 January.

Woods, P. (1985) 'Conversations with teachers: some aspects of life-history method'. *British Educational Research Journal*, **11**(11), 13–26.

Woods, P. (1986) *Inside Schools: Ethnography in Educational Research*. London: Routledge and Kegan Paul.

Woods, P. (1993) *Critical Events in Teaching and Learning*. London: Falmer Press.

Woods, P. (1999) *Successful Writing for Qualitative Researchers*. London: Routledge.

Woolgar, S. (1988) *Science: The Very Idea*. London: Tavistock.

Wright, C. (1992) *Race Relations in the Primary School*. London: David Fulton.

Yin, R. K. (1983) *The Case Study Method: An Annotated Bibliography*. Washington, DC: Cosmos.

Yin, R. K. (1984, 2nd edn, 1989) *Case Study Research: Design and Methods*. Newbury Park, Calif.: Sage. (My favourite book on the design and analysis of case studies.)

Yin, R. K. (1994) *Case Study Research: Design and Methods*. Beverly Hills, Calif.: Sage.

Youngman, M. B. (1986) *Designing and Analysing Questionnaires*. University of Nottingham: Nottingham Rediguides.

Zimmerman, D. and Wieder, D. (1977) 'The diary: diary-interview method'. *Urban Life*, **5**(4), January, 479–98.

Index